Heartfulness

Heartfulness

Robert Sardello

 GOLDENSTONE PRESS | *Gainesville, Texas*

Published by Goldenstone Press
P.O. Box 2219
Gainesville, Texas 76241
www.goldenstonepress.com

ISBN: 978-0-9967988-0-8

Edited by Lee Nichol

Cover and book design: Eva Leong Casey / Lee Nichol

Cover image: *After Rain* by Lyle Novinski

Printed in USA

Contents

HEARTFULNESS

~

Heart awareness, heartfulness, locates being fully human within the soul and spiritual center of the body, the heart. Practices of heartfulness contemplatively engage the actual organ of the heart, inwardly revealing what it is like to be incarnated in body and world. In developing the capacity to creatively radiate from the center outward, the holy, whole, nature of the human body reveals itself as intimately united with imagination, creative presence, Earth-unity, and the unfolding of the livingness of all things. It feels like our natural state, forgotten long ago.

~

＊

Heartfulness goes beyond being present to feelings, such as when we say, "I feel happy," or "I feel confused." The common meaning of "feeling" indicates the same as emotion. Feeling, in its true sense, originates in the unity between ourselves and everything visible and invisible, given as the most primary way of knowing.

＊

~

By becoming what we are present with — through the rhythms of our body, intensified most completely within the heart — we know by communion rather than by the distance of mental-ness. Artists, poets, painters, and musicians live this way of knowing, for through art we know things that cannot be known in any other way. But confining such knowing to the arts conveniently sets up the arts to be dismissed as educationally unimportant in this abstract, mental world, and also sets up feeling as specialized, rather than the most central way of being human.

~

—

Heartfulness can be lived and experienced, not just in moments of contemplation, but as sensing, perceiving, knowing, and non-causal action.

We can yield to its beckoning in any and all situations, even the most mechanical and the most technical, as well as in all relationships, and it turns the most practical work into artistic action.

Heartfulness alters what we know as power into receptive action, in harmony with the rhythms of Earth and Cosmos, from our feet to our head, from the widest expanses to the deepest interior.

No simpler "way" or "path" exists. We are not confronted with the challenge of finding heartfulness or developing it, or changing our lives in some radical manner. We are asked only to shift our center of attention, moving awareness from head to heart, from abstract cognition to being within practical contemplation, as a way of creative living.

—

＊

Such contemplative presence simultaneously beholds, embraces, and enlivens whatever we come into contact with, be it ourselves, others, nature, and even "things."

Massive programs, activism, cultural change — even if they could somehow take into account the heart — cannot do what individual heart-presence can do. Nor, however, do we imagine the multiplication of individual heart awareness gradually reaching a point of world transformation. The world in its spiritual, material, and soul essence already embraces the fullness. Heart awareness surrenders to the already-present but unknown and unlived human-world-earth completeness.

＊

In contemplative presence, whatever we notice also notices us, and the distinction between ourselves and what we notice folds into a complex and beautiful singularity in which the center, the periphery, and all between exists simultaneously as bodily feeling, knowing, and act.

Such unified presence occurs through accessing the heart, noticing that we are doing nothing more than uniting with heart-being, the contemplative center of individual life, as well as "world-being." The resonance occurring between these two centers of the Center — the Cosmos-Earth Rhythm — takes us into the primary rhythm of existence, the ongoing creation of spirit-matter-soul, and true individuality.

—

This writing addresses the "how," the "doing" of heartfulness, what can be called "method," rather than "technique." Technique consists of knowing what steps to take, and in what order, to bring about a sequence of actions leading to a desired result. Method consists of an intensification of the Whole in such a way that the Wholeness reveals itself within a resonant instance of itself. We begin with the Whole, stay with the Wholeness, and elaborate it into moments of intensity. The word "Whole" here differs from the way in which the term now abstractly runs about the world. "Wholeness" in this writing refers to the complex unity of individual-body-heart-world.

—

—

The only way into Wholeness is through the presence and preciousness of particularity. Any sensing, perceiving, or knowing devoted to the particular — rather than the general or the abstract — occurs through attentive devotion to the unique. We cannot proceed far with our abstract ideas or concepts of "heart" if we are to be within the actuality of heart. In order to be within heartfulness, we start with the actual lived presence of our heart.

We limit the way of imagining heart when we assume it to be only the anatomical organ located near the center of the chest. This "only physical" organ pumps blood through the body; we can, sometimes, feel our heart beating. Heart also refers to feeling as the emotion of love. The physical view sees heart as substance without metaphor. The emotional view sees heart as metaphor without substance. Both views abstract away from the immediacy of the experienced heart as the originating quality of bodily-felt intimate participatory awareness.

—

～

The first shifting of awareness from disembodied abstraction into presence occurs through transforming a "thought about" into attentive "presence with" — the change from "thinking about," to contemplating. Rather than thinking "about" the heart, or even thinking about "my heart," which is equally an abstraction, we instead notice what heart-presence at this place of heart is like. Only the capacity of attention-awareness can do such contemplating.

～

—

The great mystery of attention guides entry into heartfulness. It is a simple matter of "placing attention" where we intend awareness to be present, something quite different from "paying attention" to the heart. Attention acts like a very subtle spiritual substance that can "go" anywhere through the act of intent. It can even be at several places at once, simultaneously. We can, for example, place attention within the heart and within the feet at the same time.

The word "mystery" covers so much territory. Here, the "mystery" of attention does not mean unknown and unknowable, which would allow a kind of obfuscation under the guise of wisdom. Instead, "mystery" here indicates the most basic, foundational, immediately given, indivisible, actual, bodily present, spiritual, invisible, non-localized yet bodily-felt quality of awareness. Attention sweeps away with alacrity the distancing of cognitive, mental knowing.

—

~

Placing attention at the center of the heart dissolves dualistic awareness into heart awareness rather than "awareness of the heart." The latter still remains within a dualism between the inner observer and the heart as noticed from within. The former indicates a complex unity between attention and its completely united filling of the "empty form" of attention with heart awareness. It is as if attention "hovers" around and within what it attends to, permeating it in such a way that heart awareness becomes a way of presence, rather than something we are present to.

~

—

Yet, we have moved too fast, though quite deliberately so, for a rapid sweep allows a taste of what can be possible. Heart awareness alone does not constitute heartfulness, for we still feel the "encasement" within the supposed solidity of the body, and we remain as yet trapped within the body that we "know about." Within the usual awareness of our body, heart awareness cannot be sustained, for the power of "knowing about" overtakes the receptive power of pure awareness.

—

~

Correlative with the mistake of taking our awareness about the body to be the same as immediate body-awareness, comes the mistaken appearance of "the world" as something distant and removed from us — as if "in front of us," on a screen, or at most, all around us, but "objectively" removed from our being. We live within this scripted notion of existence that successfully conceals heartfulness.

Our mistaken way of experiencing body and world as "other," as if distant and removed from some unknown center, cannot be altered first, as if changing our conceptions of body and world would open the way into heart awareness. Heartfulness comes first — it is far more immediate and accessible — and gradually, we begin to notice an arriving intimacy of body and world as our habits of dualistic cognition recede.

~

~

Everyone has experienced heartfulness — perhaps a moment of awe within the natural world, or the overwhelming awakening of the heart in the presence of a newborn child, or in a passing exchange with another person, or with a work of art, music, or poetry. We feel these moments as graced, and they are, but such moments can become sustained living within primordial patterned rhythms, tones, intensities, densities, and textures of awareness — with practice.

~

～

The word "practice" itself has to be undone, taken out of its now-usual context that makes it cohere too tightly with "technique." "Practice" seems to be a kind of application of will to get something done, and with practice we get better at what we are aiming to do, gradually achieving a smooth, automatic manner rather than having to work through a sequence of activities with a kind of hyper-awareness. The "practices" that will now be introduced are not of this nature.

It may be helpful to begin with "practicing" heartfulness within an imagination of it being more like praying than practicing. Praying — as intimacy with the primordial holy body. The word "practice" carries the sense that we are out to master some challenge. Praying, if we can dispense with the connotations of religion, adequately describes the rhythmic repetition that marks living a different existence than the prosaic literalism of abstract life.

～

—

As soon we touch into heart, we find ourselves in intimate relation with invisible "presences." We do not navigate the primordial currents of the rhythmic heart alone. In fact, the most immediate, the most given sense of being within the heart consists of heart-as-holy-relation. Inherently. We thus continue "practicing," not to gain mastery, but to continually bow within the temple of primordial holy body-awareness, allowing such awareness to unfold, gradually, with its own timing, holding off our urges to get hold of what happens through naming, rather than learning the speech of the heart.

—

~

Imagine the following contemplations as gestural acts within the body-temple, rather than spiritual practices. We do them repeatedly because we do not readily rid ourselves of a kind of primordial doubt that sets up this world, this body, this heart, as "only" physical — and physical omits the spiritual-soul, conveniently putting our essence outside, someplace in the cosmos. We are asked to drop any notion of "praying to" or "praying for" anything external, and take living devotional presence as the gestural language of the heart.

~

—

Usual awareness can be characterized as scattered attention, a state of non-coherence held together by the combination of thinking and the forces of the will, with the region of the middle excluded. All head and action, plotting and doing. Our mind may be in one place, sensory attention in another place, with racing thoughts, internal tensions, moments of desire, and fleeting fantasies all happening very automatically, attention at full capture and imprisonment. Our attention remains "at attention," multi-tasking endlessly from morning to night.

—

~

The following prayer/practices — contemplating — can happen only under the condition of free forces of attention. A choice must be made to do something that has no apparent consequence, doing something without trying to get something from doing it, doing something for the sake of the doing. Such a choice opens the smallest region of light, making contemplating possible.

~

Heart Alignment

Begin, sitting quietly, eyes closed:

"Hail to the brow!" With eyes closed, place attention there, right at the center, and inwardly feel the simultaneity of expanse into an infinite sphere with unending depth, both at once, open and free, fluid. Remain here for several minutes. Remain at each phase for a few moments as it unfolds.

"Hail to the throat!" Allow attentiveness its natural flow from the brow as attention moves to the region of the throat. Notice the stillness of the brow as it moves to the throat, now felt as the most subtle inner sensation of inner movement here — as if holy speaking, silent, radiates from the region of the throat, while remaining clear and centered.

"Hail to the heart!" Allow attention to move to this center, continuing the flow from brow to throat, arriving at the place where heart-as-experienced originates simultaneous inner presence with radiance. Warmth, intimacy, unity, and circulation of sacredness are felt here. Allow attention here to flow "back" to the region of the throat and to the region of the brow, and "down again," to heart.

"Hail to the Solar Plexus!" Allow attention to move to the top of the stomach, toward the back. Notice attention here, flowing from the heart, into the very center of will. The explosive, outward "I will" — felt now as the power of pure receptivity.

Allow attention to slowly and rhythmically flow, upward through each center, and downward. These holy body centers differ from "chakras"; they are centers of aligning attention, retrieving us from scatteredness on the one hand and excessive single-centeredness on the other. Notice how we feel centered, "here," full, present, within a pervading, always-present silence as the prayer/practice concludes.

—

As the contemplation repeats daily, the servant-mind that helped us open the door toward heartfulness steps away and the contemplation becomes wholly inwardly-felt bodily gesture. This contemplation re-locates us as primordially spiritual-bodily beings. The "currents" do not stop at the region of the stomach, but continue to the very center of the Earth, and from there return in an upward coursing.

The contemplation transits into living contemplative presence as the initial "self-instruction" recedes and hands over the mantle to silently feeling the body itself come into awareness . . . attention moves to one of the centers, stays in place for a few minutes, moves to the next center, then back to each center just entered, entering into what is most primordial to the spiritual-soul human being — the rhythm of subtle light that continually enters and sustains the spiritual body . . . moving downward, in union with the rhythm of spiritual luminous darkness moving upward from the very center of the Earth.

This contemplation establishes us as "here," a "here-ness" felt from within, permeating our being, and we realize how scattered we were — and usually are — mistaking such ongoing disruption as the natural way of being.

—

~

The bodily-felt experience of the contemplation changes over time. It contains unending worlds. When the contemplation begins to feel automatic, we are actually being urged to renew the contemplative act itself. The smallest change, noticing something new within the contemplation, becomes the doorway into a different octave of our spirit-soul body-being, helping us refrain from taking this contemplation as only preliminary to heart-presence. As this contemplation changes, perhaps over years of engagement, so does heart-presence also change, unendingly.

When a contemplation ends and we open our eyes, the felt sense of the body — along with the sensory-perceptual experience of the world — becomes the most important aspect of the whole of the practice. Notice how the immediate world now appears different — more real, a feeling of unity with the surroundings, the felt experience of the interiority of all that surrounds us, the livingness of everything . . . everything as its own awareness in unity with our awareness. Such noticing may be fleeting and momentary, but sufficient to open a second unfolding toward heartfulness.

~

—

The "assembling" of our primordial being that occurs through alignment takes place within the embrace of the Silence. To feel the intensity of heart awareness and open the way to sustaining that awareness, we enter deeply into the region of primordial Silence.

The Silence can be felt through the whole of the initial contemplation, and increases as the rhythmic character of aligning occurs. Now the Silence itself opens itself and bids us to enter. Heart-presence as an actual power of receptivity cannot be fully experienced except from within the Silence.

The Silence consists of something far more extensive, intensive, and expansive than "being quiet." The Silence can be felt as a palpable presence, subtly experienced as living, bodied, and in unity with the particularity of every human world-soul-and-spirit-presence. The book, *Silence: The Mystery of Wholeness*, written by the author of these present contemplations, reveals much more concerning the Silence. Here we give only the most basic contemplative requirements for entering into the Silence — an actual, subtle region, all-permeating, within us and everything of Earth and Cosmos.

—

THE SILENCE

With eyes closed, place attention at any specific region at the periphery of the body. For example, place attention at the edge of your right arm. Notice what that feels like: it is as if you are being lightly touched by the Silence that always encompasses and embraces our bodily existence, transforming biology into spirit-soul-body presence.

Shift attention to another peripheral place of the body, such as the edge your left leg. Notice again the very palpable presence of the Silence, as if being lightly touched by an invisible, caressing presence.

Then, as you shift attention to various peripheral places of the body, notice how the Silence announces itself wherever attention occurs. You feel as if being lightly touched, subtly embraced, touched by invisibility — body relaxes, tightness eases, expansion occurs, body-awareness increases in intensity, and the existence of a new sensation occurs, the sensation of healing, of coming into Wholeness.

When noticing the Silence at the periphery of the body, feel what that is like for a while, then, at one of the bodily peripheral places, with your attention, enter into that exact region where you noticed what the Silence is like. In this act of "entering," of allowing your attention to flow into the bodily-felt silence, you identify completely with the Silence, you become the Silence. You pour your being into the Silence. What was experienced a moment ago as a subtle sensation now becomes intimately felt from within. The particular peripheral body-location of the Silence yields to an all-pervasive subtle sensing that is the presence of the Silence.

—

Attention notices the Silence through the unique way of noticing-by-resonance. The Silence already exists within and around us. By intending to place ourselves within the Silence, the resonance between the Silence within and "world-creating Silence" occurs. The Silence both surrounds , without end, and at the same time permeates without end, every aspect of our being. It feels like a vast emptiness, while simultaneously feeling as complete fullness of form.

—

~

Whenever the Silence occurs, so does alignment intensify — the feeling of bodily-soul-spirit-earth Wholeness. Alignment does not logically precede the Silence, but does so only methodologically. In the circumstances of daily living, alignment seems to be the agreement we make to enter the fullness of body-soul-spirit. We have to do something, and we make this agreement — "Yes, I will take up my life in a decidedly different way than given in the present scattering of world-existence."

~

~

The Silence can be more spontaneously experienced — as when we go walking in the mountains, or experience a sunset, or see the rays of sunlight streaming through the clouds, or when we are thrown out of usual awareness with the presence of Beauty. Within usual awareness, the Silence cannot be sustained, but shines through everything, breaking us apart at certain moments. Now, within the context of Heart Alignment, we begin to sense the true, ever-present holiness of the physical body and the physical world as inherently permeated with the Silence.

The Silence, again, consists of something more than being inwardly quiet. We speak here of "silence" as "*the* Silence," indicating an actual presence, a completely receptive, all-pervasive existence, compelling and illusive. The Silence is always here as the ground of whatever we might experience — and not just auditory sounds. Everything of the world, or Earth, comes out of the "sounding" of the Silence. Practically everyone has had an encounter with the Silence, usually in the natural world. But, it is possible to be present with the Silence under any circumstances, even in the "noisiest" places.

~

—

When we experience the Silence within the natural world, the experience fades quickly, usually as soon as we leave the place of Her appearance. This disappearance stems from the absence of awareness that experiencing anything at all requires that the Silence already exists, bodily, with us. We may think that the place we were and felt silence so strongly is, in itself, a place of silence. We are typically not aware that we already bodily exist within the Silence, but this existence makes it possible to make conscious connection with the Silence — by resonance. The intensity of inherent Silence within may well be below the threshold, and its registration requires the much stronger resonance of the Silence in the world. The recognition of this natural process inherently reveals how, with intent, sustained presence within the Silence occurs.

—

—

The ever-present Silence constitutes the medium within which heart-presence can be noticed. Heart-presence as an actual power cannot be fully experienced except from within the Silence.

—

～

Heart awareness unfolds quickly and easily from out of Heart Alignment and the Silence. Attempting to go directly into heart awareness, however, assures that cognition, the thought that one has entered into heart awareness, results. The illusion of taking thinking about heart-presence as actual presence can be strong. The best guardians of the region of the heart-as-presence are these two contemplations. Heart Alignment and the Silence are both contemplative "regions" of their own, as well as the unfolding necessary to sensory-feeling-spirit-soul-body-heart awareness.

～

GESTURING "HEART"

As the ease and comfortableness of the Silence adjust, we enter the heart through another form of resonance. We do not just go from the Silence into heart awareness.

Within the Silence, with your lips, silently gesture, speak, the word "heart." An immediate and fairly strong bodily resonating of the word occurs, and it is as if the whole of the Silence reconfigures itself as an intense, felt silence at the place of the heart.

At this place of strong bodily resonance we gently place attention within the center of the heart. Stay within the heart for as long as it remains comfortable. If anxiousness arises, try to remain within the heart, not by fighting against the anxiety, but by returning each moment to heart awareness. Complete this contemplation whenever you like. It will feel like we never want to leave.

~

Gesturing the word "heart" feels magical; it does reveal something of the magic of language. In our usual speaking, we are all nominalists. We take language to be words, and words to be agreed-upon naming, following the grammatical laws of a particular culture, used primarily to communicate. That is, words themselves are assumed to be "empty," though they convey meaning. The word "heart," gestured within the Silence. reveals, with immediacy, language-as-power and the unity of the word with the actual content of what we speak.

When we gesture "heart," no difference exists between the word and the subtle reality of heart awareness. Gesturing the word "heart" within profound silence does not point to something somewhere; the word and its reality are one. Of course, this reality of heart differs from the anatomical heart known through mental cognition.

Heart awareness, at first, feels located at the bodily region of the heart, toward the center of the chest. It is as if this region opens outward and becomes a center of radiance of what can only be called "light." Light can be felt as the action of the heart — both "light" as illumination and "light" as suddenly feeling the strength of the actual force of levity that offsets being forced into "compactness" by gravity and stress. This "light" at the same time constitutes the realm of feeling, of subtle, soul-spirit "touch." This "light-touch," while a sensory experience, does not have the same kind of limitations as other sensory experiences. While seeing, I only see; while hearing, I only hear within the hearing. While within the heart, everything becomes the felt experience of the levity of felt touch.

—

~

Notice the particular qualities of heart awareness. Let attention move around within the region of the heart. It is as if we are within a "sphere" — one, however, that has no boundaries — and what gives the quality of "concave roundness" remains mysterious but palpable. No feeling of sharp edges exists within heart awareness. We also cannot find, from within, an ending to the region of the heart. Nowhere, within heart, do we come to some kind of barrier, which when crossed, takes us out of heart. Within heart, only further expansion and depth are present.

A quality of warmth predominates here. Sometimes it even takes the form of actual heat, but always brings the warmth of intimacy. We find ourselves within intimate infinity and infinite intimacy.

~

Spend time within the heart, just noticing. Unlike other forms of contemplation or meditation, while within the heart we are not shut off from other inner experiences, though they are all now experienced as if "flowing" within the "light-touch" of feeling. Thinking can be felt — and no longer consists of "thinking-about." Emotions can be felt without being taken over by the emotion, as long as they are embraced within the light-touch of heart awareness.

When we engage the three prayer/practices of Heart Alignment, the Silence, and Heart-Awareness (forthcoming) in regular contemplations, which need not be long — fifteen minutes or so, over a period of time — it gradually becomes possible to be in any life situation and immediately enter into heartfulness, in an instant, simply by shifting attention into the heart. Heart Alignment and the Silence become more constant companions, so we do not have to stop and engage the sequence of contemplations. Heartfulness becomes available, not quite as a permanent state of being, but readily available at any time by simply placing attention within the heart. Heartfulness differs from usual consciousness in that it can never become automatic and habitual. If it were automatic, we would become, at best, automatons for the good. We remain completely free to be within heart awareness or forgetfully within usual object-awareness.

DEEPENING

~

Entering heartfulness brings new capacities of feeling and the rhythmic sense of existence into bodily, sensory, individual awareness. Engaging the prayer/practices clears the inevitable confusion of feeling with emotion. When we think of "feeling," we think of "having a feeling." Now, a more refined feeling awakens with heart awareness, something akin to intuition — the sense of knowing directly and immediately, a knowing from the "middle" rather than from the head, present in an unmistakable but usually not-quite-communicable manner. Such "intuition," when spoken, at first feels unsteady and hesitant, until this new way of knowing becomes fully trusted as a way of presence unfolding in any situation.

~

~

Heart lives the intuitive life, something much more refined than thinking. It is able to encompass what thinking attempts to do, but cannot do in its present forms of intellectualizing — that is, be one with what presents itself. Intellectualizing always performs an "about-ing" — we think "about" something. Heart becomes whatever it tends, tenderly knowing through, and as, intimacy.

~

⁓

In our current cultural milieu, non-dualism is put forth as mindfulness that does not separate itself from the known or present. Such non-dualism differs considerably from intimacy of heart, for love inheres with intuitive heartfulness. This love radiates, creates, unites, imagines, accompanies, and can be equated with conscious soul life, and indeed consists of the true essence of life itself.

Heartfulness and emotion seem to share a language universe. For every quality of heartfulness, we can also specify an emotion of the same name. Heart dimensions of joy, peace, reverence, happiness, disturbance, upset, and grief match — in name only — the emotions of joy, peace, reverence, happiness, disturbance, grief. An emotion feels like a captured feeling, taken in and possessed as if it were mine, or as if an "entity" of some sort possesses me. Both heartfulness-as-feeling and emotion, when present, completely permeate awareness. We experience emotion, though, as if coming into us — notice how suddenly we can be taken over by an emotion, suppressing the fullness of awareness, narrowing awareness to the one dimension of the emotion. We then become the emotion. Strong emotion usurps freedom.

⁓

—

Intuitive feeling — heartfulness — pervades awareness in such a manner that we experience ourselves within the feeling without losing the sense of who we are, but on the contrary, we begin living, with awareness and attention, the unfolding of who we are. It is not as though we are "already here," complete, and then fill ourselves with experiences. Rather, we are "a becoming" through the creating activity of the action of love, through the heart. The center of our being now becomes heart-centered. Individuality pervades the feeling without obscuring feeling in any way, and feeling does not obscure the sense of the I, but bodies it in full individuality. Heartfulness lives within and enlivens the preciousness of individuality, while gradually exposing the illusion and falseness of egotism.

—

Both intuitive feeling and emotion occur bodily. Emotion occurs as the excitation of body processes — the expansion or contraction of the blood vessels, glandular secretions, reactions of the viscera. Consciousness, under the onset of emotion, refuses its normal functions. The unique preciousness of the person vanishes and we give ourselves over to primal powers that now explode without guidance.

Heartfulness radiates through the body and we become complete in our presence, and thus complete in presence with others and world. Our central being, our individuality, intensifies rather than diminishes, but never in a self-possessive way. Individuality orients completely toward radiant giving.

—

Heartfulness needs the repetition and unfolding of prayer/practices. The prayer/practices give form a starting place, a small window into intuitive feeling. Rhythmic repetition of prayer/practices does not "strengthen" the soul or the forces of will. The notion of the strengthening of the will makes the soul sound like she does muscular workouts to get stronger. Heartfulness does not unfold in such a manner, and in fact unfolds in an opposite way. Heart unfolds to the extent that we yield to receptivity, a kind of surrender. But, we cannot "do" surrender. We cannot will to surrender; we can only allow it or disallow it when it beckons. Heartfulness beckons, more and more intensely, releasing forms that have no life, such as automatic habits of thinking, reactive emotions, mental wanderings, and judgments. Heartfulness occurs more as an "undoing" rather than a "doing." The next undoing, taking us even deeper into heartfulness, concerns the loosening of the body felt as encasement, and the opening of body as awareness.

—

Conceptual, abstract, intellectual thinking does not follow the laws of the heart, so our first "opening into receptivity" concerned gently noticing attention within the heart, rather than the automatic residence of attention in the region of the head. A new range of receptive intimacy, in clarity of intuitive awareness, heart-centered, begins to open.

We notice, though, that intuitive heart awareness recedes very quickly. The comparatively hard and brittle qualities of living a *conception* of the body, rather than *within* body, take over. Because we live the illusion of the body understood in only one way — that of being a physiological, biological, biochemical, medical thing — awareness within heart counters what we think we know. Heart, in her pure receptivity, goes along, in surrender, with this literalism of body, in a way, allowing herself to be trapped.

Just as we began with the necessary illusion of a physical-biological heart and undid the illusion by entering into the immediacy of trusting experience, we now allow depth to take place by an undoing of the intellectual concept of body-as-thing. "Heart-as-presence" and "body-as-thing" set up a dissonance that must be resolved.

Heart-Awareness

Heart as center of intuitive feeling-awareness, even when experienced for but a few moments, begins to dissolve the resistances of conceptualizing, which occur as taking our bodily being literally — "Well, it is only a physical, physiological thing, and that's all of it." Can a literal, physical, physiological thing do this?:

Take a flower, but one that is not particularly beautiful or outstanding in any way, an ordinary flower, and carefully observe it. (After working with a flower for several weeks, you can change to something else — a stone, for example.) Hold the flower in your hand and look at it with tending care, turning it over, seeing it from all sides. After doing this observation for a few minutes, make an inner image of the flower.

At first it is likely that this will be a mental image of the flower. You can tell it if is a mental image if you "see" the flower with your interior eye as if you are looking at the flower; that is, you mentally see only one side of the flower.

Allow the image to move down into the interior of your heart; that is, now "see" the flower with the heart's eye. You will have the feeling of seeing all sides of the flower at once, something like a hologram. It is not a literal "seeing," but more like feeling — a felt, but quite precise sense of the flower, occurring within the heart as feeling that is like a "seeing."

Simply hold the flower in heart awareness, for a few minutes . . . Then, consciously erase the image of the flower and remain in the empty void as long as you can. Then open your eyes.

This contemplation enacts a surrendering to the nature and laws of the imaginal heart, the heart of felt substance and the substance of felt heart, breaking through our literalized notions of the heart as a substance without metaphor and a metaphor without substance.

~

This prayer/practice accustoms us to sensing feeling-presence, its particularity and accuracy. When done in a regular manner, we gradually remain longer within heart-feeling, with deeper awareness in a more sustained way. A transformative process of more subtle embodiment initiates, one of great importance, not only because it begins the freeing of the encasement of body-as-thing, but also because the form of awareness which accompanies such encasement — egotism — quiets somewhat.

~

~

Notice how the heart-feeling of the flower clearly interiorizes the flower, but interior here does not mean "inside." The actual experience of the heart-feeling of the flower feels as if it occurs as a kind of dimensional space that exists simultaneously "around" us and "within" us. We feel both within the flower, and the flower within us.

Heart-feeling cannot be put into the rubrics of mental consciousness without touching off the self-preservation activity of ego-awareness. What we experience with the flower consists of something far more than a momentary lapse of usual awareness. Until we feel, through and through, that this very simple practice opens noticing that we are always living in another dimension than the third dimension, but we were not aware of its presence — until then, sustained heart awareness cannot come about.

~

In order to gradually inhabit this newly experienced dimension, notice that ego awareness consists of something more than the highly sketchy word, "consciousness." We assume that this habitual state characterizes "us," belongs to us as "ours." Actually, ego consciousness has an autonomous life, one that throws us into a comfortable ease of functioning with extremely minimal awareness. And should this awareness be threatened, the autonomous aspects of ego consciousness — doubt and fear — come into play as its most potent protectors. A feeling of doubt then crawls around the edges of heartfulness, trying to dispel it as illusory.

It is as if we are "allowed" moments of coming to the door of already-present but unnoticed dimensions of awareness — as long as these qualities of intimacy and unity seem as if illusory moments, or at best ephemeral, like dreams — while what we now inhabit as awareness has solidity and permanence and functionality and practicality. Doubt thus prevents noticing other present and more primordial dimensions, and fear accompanies doubt as its companion protector, shutting down what tries to open us up. We easily miss heartfulness when it is attacked by doubt and fear. Doubt and fear are dissolved by being exposed for what they are. Doing so, this habitual consciousness backs down and allows us to go on, go deeper, proceed further into heart. And the truth of heart awareness can continue its awakening.

When the above insight takes hold, really takes hold, that is, somehow slips by or through the "keepers of ordinariness," then, quite suddenly, in an instant, we notice heart experience begins to be more sustainable. The region of the heart can even be strongly bodily felt, as if a center of awareness, heart awareness, rather than awareness-of-the-heart. A primary characteristic of heartfulness now also reveals itself — the very strongly felt sense of being body rather than "having a body." This characteristic truly inaugurates heartfulness as the proper and natural mode of human awareness, while revealing the trickiness of the very amazing and useful, but wholly secondary mode of ego consciousness.

~

The prayer/practice just described, Heart-Awareness, can be entered at any moment once Heart Alignment and the Silence become comfortable experiences. The practice can be done anywhere, and needs to be, for something else of great importance begins to be felt — the true nature of intuitive heart awareness as *rhythmic*. The natural world, in particular, lives and comes into being every moment through rhythm. We experience rhythm everywhere in the natural world — day/night, seasons, life/death, days, weeks, months, years, as well as body rhythms such as the primary rhythm of the heart and the rhythms of digestion. Movement too occurs rhythmically.

Often we do not experience these primordial, ever-present creating rhythms, for ego awareness occurs digitally rather than rhythmically. When within ego consciousness, we see something or we do not; we sense something or we do not, we think this and not that. Flow does not exist for ego. But the trickiness of ego consciousness makes us believe we experience continuity. Fear arises the moment the continuity of the known undergoes disturbance.

To be present within heart awareness, without unknowingly importing usual consciousness as a kind of overlay, the prayer/practice just presented needs to become something like a "heart-mantra." Gradually, the sense of heart awareness as "rhythm-awareness" can be felt. However, such presence of rhythm differs from what we consciously notice as rhythm, such as in music. And, it differs also from what we sometimes feel as the rhythm of the pulse or the heartbeat. These are all sensory/cognitive registrations of rhythm, rhythm from the "outside." What is the interior sense of rhythm?

—

—

Intuitive heart-rhythm-awareness consists of a very deeply-felt sense that everything, even what presents itself to sensory experience and perception as static, lives within rhythm. This quality can hardly be described in its subtleness. A tree, for example, which looks as if static, can be felt rhythmically. The periodicity of its rhythm seems to extend over a long period of time — the season of spring through summer, into fall and then winter, and then again into spring. We know that rhythm exteriorly. We can also begin to imagine it interiorly, and even begin to feel such rhythm bodily, when we perceive the tree from within heart. The knowing and remembering of rhythm in the outward manifestation dims when feeling rhythm within the heart, and instead subtle "surging" and "ebbing" can be felt within the heart and even throughout the body.

When noticing the tree in this manner, feeling a bodily unity with what stands before us, smaller sensed rhythms open inwardly. It helps to sense rhythm by noticing the small movements of nature — such as when a breeze moves the leaves, we can feel the rhythmic movement as belonging to the life of the tree rather than caused by the wind. When we see birds lighting for a moment, flying to a branch, then returning to the ground, we can feel the tree in its rhythm with who visits it. The felt sense of such occurrences gradually extends to all that exits, but can only be noticed through intuitive heart awareness. Interiorly, rhythm occurs as felt pulsations of opening and contraction.

⁓

~

Rhythmic attentiveness increases gradually as the body we presently live begins to physiologically change. We do not train the mind to notice rhythms, but invite body presence to swim in the deliciousness of world creation, of which we are not only a part, but are a key feature — the intuitive awareness feature — without which creation too appears done and finished, and then we live in entropic decline.

~

~

Without some form of gentle, ongoing prayer/practice, heart awareness quickly descends into a process coming to premature completion. Mentalizing takes over. We then also descend into another form of egotism — the egotism of the sentimental, emotional, "me-centered" heart, now disguised as spiritual development.

~

＿

Transforming the center of presence from head to heart coordinates body-awareness with a transformation of world presence. Here we have the most significant and unique and necessary changes brought about through heartfulness. As we transform, so does the world. The commonly promoted notion of "change ourselves first, and then go out and change the world" simply does not work, except at a horizontal level, meaning that our own being, even though we go through some kind of training, remains essentially the same as before — in substance. We might well develop a felt urgency to now bring change into the world and seek given and available ways to do so. The kind of transformations described here are much more radical, leading to contemplative action rather than dividing contemplation from action.

＿

—

As the prayer/practice of noticing heart-world-rhythm develops, we come to a built-in verification process of the power of heart. As we change, the world changes, and such changes can be readily noticed from within heart awareness. Changes occur in such a manner that we notice the polarity of body-awareness with world presence — both at once. Such polarity of noticing verifies something actually taking place. We have not projected some "unconscious" fantasy onto the world. A moment of a kind of "inner click" occurs. The rhythm of heart awareness with sensing/perceiving does not shock us, nor do we suddenly feel psychotic or delusional or afraid. We feel the exact process occurring. The onset of the changes occur as awakenings, rather than as some kind of imposition that threatens.

—

—

Heart centers us within bodily freedom as changes occur within, rather than being governed by external forces. The changes occur gradually, and require consciously altering attention that still goes on as captured by whatever engages us at the moment. However, a small, inner "space" now exits, and it becomes possible to shift attention from the "space of the usual," into heart awareness. This conscious heart engagement, going to the heart deliberately, immediately results in feeling our awareness move to the center of the chest, and a "circle" of radiance issuing from that region. The immediacy and closeness, the intimacy of this felt center, can be likened to a "signature" of our being as true; up to this point, without knowing it, we had been living as lurkers to the world.

—

～

Heart-awakening gradually becomes a new mode of knowing ourselves and world as a complex unity. We might call this kind of presence "Completeness." We feel, exactly and precisely, complete — as precious and whole individuals in ongoing intimate presence with world, given also as precious and whole.

～

~

Heartfulness cannot be sustained as the center of ongoing awareness unless accompanied by also noticing body-as-sensing. Within the intimated and felt completeness, heart's radiance spreads through bodily being — it can indeed be felt doing so. It becomes more important, then, to notice the tingling and surging of currents occurring, than to curtail the bodily transformation by basking in the awe of immediate heart experience. Notice the world, nature, others, notice from the region of the heart, bodily so. If we only notice what happens to us — how we feel more present, filled with a kind of warmth, more intimate with the world, open in the realm of feeling — then we have only discovered a new form of egotism, and we capture heart for ourselves.

~

~

In earlier times, the training to become an alchemist began with several years of simply noticing sensations. Alchemy perhaps has to be "de-literalized," taken out of the notion of strange individuals in smelly laboratories attempting to turn lead into gold. They were engaged in transforming the heaviness of body — physical-ness as "only physical" — into the golden light of heart. We can now be doing this transforming all the time, as the labor of heart-speaking occurs within the laboratory of the world.

~

Sensory Heart-Awareness

The awakening of body as soul-spirit-physical that takes place through heartfulness continues its unfolding through heart-sensing. Sensing becomes whole, it becomes the act of the forming of the soul-body, rather than having a physical body peppered with the senses. The encased physical body simply lives as if there are numerous "peep holes" into the outer world, the senses as physiological mechanisms for registering what exits "out there" as "over here," at any moment. Such a view severely contradicts the living experience of heartfulness.

We enter a new life, and it has to cohere. Slipping in and out of heartfulness at our convenience does not work. When within heartfulness, notice the accompanying "sense-fulness." For example, you might begin with noticing sound:

Begin by noticing heartfulness through aligning, opening into the Silence, and gesturing the word "heart." Then, allow the usual awareness of sound to be felt as sound-awareness by noticing something, such as a bird singing or the clank of something metal, move from its seeming location at the place of the ears, to also moving outward from the heart-awakened body, toward the source of what you hear. You hear a bird singing; you allow the rhythmic sound to also be felt as if originating from the heart-awakened body toward the bird, and back. This prayer/practice, as with each of the prayer/practices, simply notices the actual happening — in this case of sound. We do not try to make something happen with the prayer/practices, but rather take up now an ongoing unfolding of tuning our new embodiment.

We might also do this prayer/practice by getting a small chime or bell, and daily, doing the prayer/practice of sounding. Begin noticing how completely unconscious we typically remain to the actual bodily process of sensing. With the sounding, the usual sensing of sound — as if we are "here" and the sound occurs "over there," and has to come "into" our physical body — transforms. We notice a radiance of heart through the body in such a way that when sound happens, we do not "hear" sound, but rather we are sound, we have become sound.

～

This prayer/practice can be done with any mode of sensing — sight, touch, taste, warmth, smell, and the rest of sensing, now given as Sensory Heart-Awareness, rather than sensing *of* something. Prayerful sensing also sustains and intensifies heartfulness, as we notice body awakening itself. This awakening astounds, for it does not originate from any outside force. Body, in our usual sense of body, remains confined to being subject to everything outside itself. There seems to be no freedom in being bound to body. Now, bodily freedom begins to awaken.

The important dimension of the prayer/practice lies in simultaneously noticing body in union with world. These prayers are not about "us," not in the usual way we engage in such strong looking for what some action can do for the "me." As long as noticing of heartfulness occurs with this unity-in-duality, usual egotism recedes; its return signals the dimming of heartfulness.

～

Within Sensory Heart-Awareness, what do things look like? Or does seeing become so intimate that you do not "see" so much as you "are" the seeing and the seen? We notice that the sounding space or the hearing space, that which we usually apprehend as "thin" and empty, now feels substantial, as if it can be touched, felt. Colors blend into the substance-space, not completely leaving where they inhere, but no longer so self-enclosed as things with color, for the surrounding space can be felt as also the inner space of the heart.

Perhaps you wonder what may be happening to you. This unfolding takes place at a pace and rhythm that does not throw us into apprehension or fear. Still, usual, distanced, cognitive awareness typically remains so strong that we do not realize that we live in this distanced way. We do not trust immediate experience. Immediate experience seems like illusion, when in fact we now live illusory existence because it is all mediated and we long for intimacy.

At the edges of consciousness, an ongoing anxiousness reveals that we live a separated and isolated existence, but we cannot find the way out. The way out is the way of "Yes," the way of yielding. The "Yes" feels the support of the emerging feeling of now belonging to a holy Earth-Cosmos. The clue to the validity of what now happens does not lie in the wonder or the awe or the unusualness, but in the immediacy of a sense of completeness. Completeness everywhere, and always very particular, very specific — not some generalized notion.

—

A Momentary Diversion . . .

Experiencing heartfulness as readily present, while at the same time slipping readily back into a "distanced" view to the world and others, leaves a remaining air of subtle doubt. Does this process of development take us into the depths of reality or into just another construction? Such discomfort, when consciously allowed, opens further and deeper engaging with heart and body. A purification process now beckons. Here, the doubt is not so much the forces of usual consciousness exerting their superiority, but a moment of decision. If an inward "Yes," cannot be felt, if *cour-age* of heart does not come forth, the moment can turn into a rejection of the whole process.

Nothing exits in our present culture demonstrating the human body as simultaneously "soul-spiritual-bodying-worlding" unfolding. Existence within the world of nouns— everything as completed — only appears to dissolve itself through a hyper-speeding-up of the world-as-noun-things, brought about primarily though making the illusory world even more illusory through digitalizing.

This speeding up of the world creates the illusion of an animated, living world. But in fact, such pseudo-animation turns Earth into a mechanism. We know this process is now underway, and the more we perceive Earth as a mechanism, the more we — the "perceivers" — also become mechanized. Our engagement with the heart as the center of soul-spirit-body-earth thus cannot find anything outside itself to verify its reality. And, since heartfulness has not yet found its way to continuity, too many and too-frequent gaps occur. The daily advances of the digitalized world exert their dazzling power, and we find ourselves becoming intelligent mechanisms with heart-longing. This heart-longing too will be lost, gone and without remembrance.

The intent of heartfulness does not lie in standing against the emerging world mechanisms, for that would only indicate being caught by them — and the capacity of true freedom is then already completely usurped. The remarkable and daily advances of mechanistic-digitalized world-animation occurring through outside forces — rather than the animating of being characteristic of soul — provide the necessary urgency of our longing to be whole and complete spiritual-moral human beings. This illusory world may make heartfulness more difficult, but it also inspires the felt necessity of meeting any and all difficulties with inner presence.

With heartfulness we open to a body-world unity as inherently moral. "Moral" here simply means that not only our actions but our consciousness, our awareness, results in something happening in the world, and we are thus responsible for our awareness. The opening of heart capacities reveals something much more, much deeper than just another possible way that we can unfold as human beings. We cannot place our efforts on a kind of horizontal plane that seems as if we are offered two choices — digital-mechanical existence or heartfulness — of meeting the future. What constitutes the essential nature of the difference between these two ways of being? Is it efficiency? Or comfort? Power? Technological acumen?

Setting up the choice in any of these ways would mean we have not yet touched into the irreplaceable feel of heart-presence . . . an inhering unfolding of life as moral — moral given as immediate bodily feeling and heart sensation. World-as-mechanism thus lacks, terribly, in efficiency, for moral becomes reduced to "morality," given as external forces of religion, ethics, or jurisprudence. The inherent moral nature of heart awareness incorporates all of the soul qualities that as yet remain objectivized in external institutions. As institutionalized, they are subject to being formed and reformed as mechanisms themselves — they leave less and less room for human individuality and creativity.

Having now touched on the critical issues of doubt, courage, mechanistic social forces, and morality, we can return to the main thread of the work.

Pure Body-Awareness

The prayer/practices awaken noticing how our body does not exist as an objective thing, but as the inherent way of being earthly sources of unified life and awareness. An accompanying relief, from the correlative assumption of the world as "already there, and completed," now can intensify through developing Pure Body-Awareness.

How we are world-present determines what we notice as present. When we live within the assumption of body-as-encased — and the encasement holds complex anatomy and physiology, understood through medicine and the sciences — then the world inevitably appears as a multiplicity of "encased" objects, or processes-as-only-material activity. As we open to heartfulness, we do so within this habit of bodily existence. The two — heartfulness and anatomical, physiological body — clash, with the far more habitual way of physical being ruling.

Heartfulness lives, thrives, and expands within "body-fulness." The boundaries of body do not stop at the skin. Awareness of the body transforms easily into body-awareness through a prayer/practice of Pure Body-Awareness:

As with all prayer/practices, begin by sitting in a quiet place where you will not be disturbed, and close your eyes.

Begin this practice by doing the Heart Alignment and shifting your awareness to the place of the heart. Then, go into the Silence. Let your attention notice the area surrounding your body. Feel the presence of the currents of the Silence, which are like being gently touched, felt at the body periphery.

When you feel these currents, switch your attention to the interior of your body, to the interior space of the body, to the currents of the Silence there. This feels as if the interior is an empty, but substantial space. The Silence within the interior of the body is qualitatively different than the Silence surrounding and penetrating the body. It is deeper, much deeper, endlessly deep, whereas the Silence surrounding the body has the quality of infinite expanse.

When you have that sense of the interior of the Silence of the body, switch your attention again to the outside surrounding your body. With your attention, switch back and forth a number of times. At first, this "switching" is difficult. If it does not feel difficult, then it is likely that you are doing the "switching" only mentally. When you switch from interior to exterior and back, it has to be done bodily; that is, when you "intend" the switch, you also feel it resonating bodily. You can feel that this is an effort of the receptive will, rather than simply "thinking about it."

When the switching has occurred several times, dissolve the feeling of the presence of a thin "membrane" separating interior and exterior currents of the Silence, and you are within Pure Body-Awareness. The boundary of the skin as encasing body seems removed, and yet no sense of being "out of body" results. We feel completely bodied, and yet do not experience the bounded form of our body.

—

While we cannot live permanently within this kind of body-awareness, and falling into habitual body sense occurs, at the same time an inner, felt, "knowing" affirms that the prayer/practice touches into something very real; no illusory trick takes place. When we exist within mental awareness, body presents as bounded form, accompanied by what we have been told about anatomy and physiology. Aches and pains occur even within the depths of the organs, and seem to verify a three-dimensional body as "the" reality of whose physical interior we have but an inkling.

Within Pure Body-Awareness, bounded form cannot be felt unless we fall into a thought about our body in a usual sense. Body freedom initiates, even if it cannot be sustained. This body — the body-of-life — while corporeal, has no visibility, defying the known laws of the physical world. Yet we feel, if anything, much more a part, a dimension of the physical world, deeply entwined and yet free — not as a "mental" sense of freedom, but rather, bodily-experienced freedom from impingements from "outside" forces.

—

～

Pure Body-Awareness sustains for a short time. Notice that within this awareness, the world, Earth, things, creatures, others, feel united with Pure Body-Awareness, while retaining known forms. It is as if we experience more of, further dimensions of, world. Pure Body-Awareness accompanies heartfulness, and can be noticed even without this prayer/practice, though through the prayer/practice the experience intensifies considerably.

～

—

At least for a little while, we can notice the extraordinary experience of being wholly corporeal and yet invisibly united with whatever we might sense. Cognition and perceiving do not disappear — through these capacities we still see, for example, a tree "over there." At the same time we feel completely united with the tree, and the tree with us. Or we notice, with immediacy, the invisible qualities of another person in a kind of intimacy of presence that does not interfere at all with the autonomy of the person, but rather enhances it, because the usual "wall" between ourselves and another does not exist in this dimension.

—

—

After a time of engagement with heartfulness, any of the prayer/practices can be made into a kind of an attention-mantra within the Great Silence. Unlike a mantra consisting of repeating spoken or inner words, through "mantra attention" we can shift in and out of Heart Alignment, the Silence, Heart-Awareness, and Pure Body-Awareness. As the awareness deepens and intensifies, something akin to walking along the street and then going into a church or a temple becomes familiar, whenever attention orients toward heartfulness.

—

~

Awareness, body, heart, world-presence, presence with others and the presence of others with us, go considerably beyond anything capable of description in non-qualitative language. It is as if we notice the habitual, purely physical body as well as the spiritual body, enfolding into one unified complexity that opens only through attention and through heart-presence.

~

—

Each new attentiveness that arrives through a prayer/practice in turn folds into a previously developed awareness and opens to an ongoing sense of "becoming," rather than being formed as a human being by everything that has happened in the past. Heart knows only the present, the extended "now," because heart awareness coincides completely with time-awareness. The body of three dimensions does not live wholly within those dimensions; it is encompassed by living-time, the fourth dimension. This time has no relation to clock time, which segments continuity into measurable units. The fourth dimension can be felt as something like an unending and unbounded spacious continuity.

—

—

Within heartfulness and the unbounded body, in intimacy with the unfolding coming-into-creation world, and with others as mysteries revealed each moment, we come into being aware within the dimension of time. This "time" does not go from past to present and toward the future, but it is time as bodied and living, experienced so completely that who we are, and our living as time-beings, coincide as vivified world-soul presences.

—

Pure Body-Awareness begins to both accompany heartfulness, and also alter it considerably. When within this mode of awareness, if we gesture the word "heart," an immediate resonance of heart-presence occurs, a resonance much stronger than when we gesture "heart" from within the Silence alone. Gesturing from within the Silence, as was suggested earlier, only implies world-presence. The resonance seems to "stay" within a kind of bodily vibratory quality. When we gesture "heart" from Heart-Awareness, it feels as if the resonance of heart starts from a deep center-point, radiates out through the body, and continues, without perceptible conclusion.

The radiance of the heart certainly does not occur in linear or horizontal fashion, as the description here might imply. While occurring, at least for a long while, it feels as if we are not quite able to experience the process in all its detail. It is not so much that attention lacks. Rather, we do not hold any given inner memory form that would in-form what occurs.

～

Gradually allowing more and more intensity of heartfulness requires refraining from both the "desire to know about," and the "desire for the ineffable." Either or both forms exert themselves, and the never-ending unfolding of heartfulness stops when the resonance becomes tinged with the desire for something like religious experience. Feeling satisfied in either or both of these ways begins the formation of a kind of mystical egotism, one that may well be more dangerous than the present egotisms that abound — more dangerous because they disguise themselves as "new forms" with which to be more vividly present. The moment the "forming" gets cognized as a set form, we seem to at last be on the way toward a "new world," when in fact we are rolling around in a variation of what we are trying to heal. We are back to a place prior to where we began working in this manner, without realizing that has happened.

～

A propensity to turn the realm of the inherent feeling-heart into typical familiarities haunts our dedication and devotion. The tendency cannot be stopped except by exposing it, which deflates its considerable power. One might feel, for example, "Well, if this does not go anywhere, if it cannot be simplified and made into something practical and easy, something that I can add on to who I know myself to be, then I want no part of it." Or, "If this heart work really requires the kind of attentiveness and tending that I'm beginning to get a sense of, it just won't fit into the kind of life I'm required to live." These kinds of reactions, and many more besides, expose how deeply bound we really remain. These kinds of reactions also bring trying to live life as a set of conclusions to question.

Usual awareness re-asserts itself over and over again in large measure because we have not yet explicitly included the sacred heart-presence of other people. We have begun where heartfulness does appear more readily, which prepares us for heart-listening.

Heartfulness
as Permanent Presence

～

When the prayer/practices deepen, we know exactly the moment when they reveal themselves as something we have taken in from outside, as yet another aspect of our lives. This moment is critical, for we have taken on something given as a set of "practices." There comes a time when the prayer/practices reveal themselves in and as a deeper dimension than "instructions." The experience of that moment can occur with any of the prayer/practices, and is the moment when we fully awaken inwardly and discover the prayer/practices as freeing us rather than binding us.

We notice that the practices function neither as a means to accomplishing some desire to live differently, nor what someone claims to be the "next thing" to try that will make life meaningful. *The prayer/practices begin to reveal themselves as actual spiritual presences.* These holy presences inhere within the wording and the experiencing. Careful tending and noticing within the space of waiting and listening reveals that these "practices," these words, have an autonomy; they exist in union with us, and open to, or as, felt spiritual presences.

～

Heartfulness tends toward being incorporated as a variation of other forms of meditation or contemplation. The analogies with the contemplative mystic, or the current emphasis on mindfulness, have probably occurred to you. We often hear in the classes on heartfulness that heartfulness seems very "Buddhist." I have also taught in a center where the great Christian contemplative tradition now continues in a more public way. I was easily understood there, but that understanding occurred through the pre-understanding of the mystical tradition. Hearing through an already-given framework restricts what can be heard. Heartfulness does not have its home in either Buddhism or the Christian contemplative tradition — not if "tradition" is understood as of the past, or the inherence of the past as living in the present. These two senses of "tradition" do not open the possibility of the radically new, a newness that can re-open aspects of spiritual traditions in new ways, allowing the unknown to move now from the future into the present, rather taking the past as a template of the present and the future.

Rather than an attempt to find life as holy and whole, heartfulness helps us notice that life and world are already Whole. It is thus closer to the Wisdom tradition than to spiritual or religious traditions.

~

The soul-movement of the prayer/practices introduced thus far can, with one further prayer/practice, enter into the world. This prayer/practice occurs as a kind of pregnant, living harmony of all the practices, occurring now as a kind of symphony, of which we have been learning the notes. The symphonic uniting of these practices makes moving to the next octave of the heart far easier than trying to add on more.

When I was in Assisi, Italy, and our group was doing the various heart contemplations in the context of the presence of the living aura of St. Francis, how he experienced the world came alive. It is as if what he practiced every day — the practice of relinquishing everything, the practice of living from heart in the midst of the world, dedication to Lady Poverty, allowing everything to be taken away, daily — came into a living synthesis as his "Canticle of the Creatures":

St. Francis — Canticle of the Creatures

Most high, all powerful, good Lord!
All praise is yours, all glory, all honor, all blessing.

To you alone do they belong.
No mortal lips are worthy to pronounce your name.

Be praised, my Lord, through all your creatures,
But especially through my lord Brother Sun, who brings the day.
You give light through him.
He is beautiful and radiant in all his splendor!
Of you, Most High, he bears the likeness.

Be praised, my Lord, through Sister Moon and the stars.
You have made them bright and precious and beautiful.

Be praised, my Lord, through Brothers Wind and Air,
and clouds and storms and all else,
Through which you give your creatures sustenance.

Be praised, My Lord, through Sister Water.
She is useful, and humble, and precious, and pure.

Be praised, my Lord, through Brother Fire,
Through whom you brighten the night.
He is beautiful and cheerful, and full of manly strength.

Be praised, my Lord, through our sister Mother Earth, who feeds us and
rules us, and gives us fruits with colored flowers, and grass.

Be praised, my Lord, through those who forgive by way of love for you,
Through those who endure sickness and trial.

Happy are those who endure in peace, for through you,
Most High, they will be crowned.

Be praised, my Lord, through our Sister Bodily Death,
From whose embrace no one living can escape.
Woe to those who die in sin, happy those she finds doing your most holy will.
No second death can do them harm.

Oh, praise my Lord, and bless my Lord, and thank my Lord!
Serve him with great humility . . .

～

Francis was able to experience, directly and immediately, that all of the world consists of creating beings that are so intimate with us that we usually take them for granted as "always here," and yet separate from us — a knowing that casts these presences into "the already known," and thereby distancing them from our heart.

Francis here relates how he experiences the whole of the world as spiritual presences. Such noticing turns life into ongoing ritual action — not ritual as a completed form, but the act of "ritual-ing," of feeling everything as constantly coming into form, as if for the first time.

～

"Sealing" Heart-Awareness

We come now to a similar juncture with the prayer/practices of the heart. We do so by "sealing" each of the heart practices into one symphony. "Sealing" here does not mean "closing off" by putting a kind of "stamp" on the prayer/practices, but, rather holding now all the prayer/practices within the heart simultaneously, which will allow us to move into the world without trying to figure out which practice would be most important at any given moment.

Do the Heart Alignment prayer/practice. Then "seal" it by gesturing the words "Brother Heart Alignment."

These words resonate deeply and strongly within the subtle body, and the Heart Alignment resonates through the body, moving down the centers as when inwardly speaking each step. Then, the next time you are going to do the Heart Alignment, you just gesture the words "Brother Heart Alignment," noticing how the whole alignment happens without having to go through the entire process. It is the presences that were doing the aligning all along, but we were not yet receptive enough to notice, and instead thought that we were "doing something," rather than invoking the help of spiritual presences.

Then, from time to time, to check up and strengthen the whole, do the entire Heart Alignment as described earlier, followed by gesturing the words, "Brother Heart Alignment." Otherwise, after a while, the mind does its tricky thing and the sealing gesture reverts to being only outer words lacking interior resonance.

While all of the prayer/practices presented thus far are crucial, once a level of comfort with them occurs, so that we are no longer "self-instructing" ourselves in order to feel what the practices are doing, then these key prayer/practices can be "sealed", as indicated with the Heart Alignment. The sealing can be developed in the following way:

Do each of the prayer/practices, followed with gesturing these words:

Heart Alignment — "Brother Heart Alignment"

The Silence at the periphery of the body — "Sister Silence"

The Silence within the interior of the body — "Brother Silence"

Pure Body-Awareness — "Brother-Sister Pure Body-Awareness"

Heart-Awareness — "Sister Heart-Awareness"

—

If each instance of the naming of the presences in this way does not result in bodily feeling the exact qualities that occur when doing the extended prayer/ practices, then the moment of sealing has not yet arrived. Continue with the longer way of doing the prayer/practices, returning from time to time to try the sealings.

Even when the sealing can be fully felt, still, from time to time go back and do all of the practices stated thus far. Doing so is a bit like doing basic finger practices with a piano. No matter how advanced a pianist becomes, these basic practices have to be returned to again and again. A wonderful violinist once told me, "When I don't practice for one day, I notice it the next day. When I don't practices two days in a row, some people notice it in my playing. When I don't practice for three days in a row, everyone notices it."

—

HEARTFULNESS WITH OTHERS

～

Nearly all forms of meditation and contemplation remain individually oriented, and the prevailing wisdom says that through the individual, world change perhaps occurs. With heartfulness, however, individual contemplation forms but the first phase of a continuous unfolding of spheres of heartfulness. The "second sphere" of heartfulness concerns heart-presence with others. This sphere involves more than applying heartfulness, once developed, to our relating with others. The prayer/practices we are about to enter are not applications, but originating, new forms of relating — embodied, spirit-soul, heart-relating.

As with all realms of true feeling — such as music, poetry, or art — the foundations are never left behind. Individual heart contemplation remains essential, even as further heartfulness worlds open; it remains the source point of emerging new capacities. We never master heart contemplation, but it does become possible to be always close in attentiveness to the heart, and heartfulness can, with the slightest shifting of attention, occur almost instantly. The prayer/contemplations described thus far also continue to deepen and expand in unending ways.

～

—

The power of receptivity, and heart as the central organ of receptivity, gradually can become our way of life. The words "power" and "receptivity" do not seem to go together. Our conception of power remains much more of the "push" and of the "explosive" variety of qualities. The effort of getting something intended actually done, remains our usual sense of power. Receptivity may be "nice," but it does not seem able to "do anything." At best, it seems a respite from a world based almost entirely in the "I will," "I do" sense of power.

—

—

An immense difference exists between will power and receptivity. While contemplation in the mystical tradition involves receptivity to the presence of God, and mindfulness involves receiving whatever happens in life without reaction, in calmness and a kind of loving detachment, heartfulness receives all of the world as a "temple of presences."

—

⁓

I recently attempted to describe "world-as-temple" to a friend who follows a Native American tradition. When he goes into the sweat lodge, he leaves the outer world and goes into a temple of receptivity. It is a special "precinct" where one communes with spiritual presences. One experiences power there, but only by being receptive, not by trying to willfully accomplish something. When the sweat concludes and he steps outside the lodge, he enters, again, the outer world of power, hoping to retain some sense of receptiveness to the elemental spirits of Earth and sky, plants and animals, and others. Something similar occurs in entering any "temple" — a church or synagogue, in meditation or contemplation. *But with heartfulness, we are always within the "temple."* We do not have to seek the temple, but only the attentiveness necessary to experience it. This first "sphere," then, notices the temple at the very core — the individual heart. As the *cour-age* of heart unfolds, we then enter a second sphere of heartfulness — the sphere of the always-present shared heart.

This second sphere of heartfulness begins to alter completely the usual qualities of power, and also reveals how heartfulness really does something, though it always occurs through the quality of a "non-doing-doing." We might also call this receptive form of power "heart-empathy," as it occurs in our relating with others — though a qualification exists in utilizing a word like "empathy," for empathy only forms an opening into this sphere.

We begin by becoming comfortable with the first sphere of heartfulness as inherently a way of noticing the spiritual qualities, and adjusting to entering those qualities all the time, everywhere. Even if they are not our immediate focus, they can be felt around us as a kind of palpable "aura," and simultaneously within us as a kind of velvety inner substantial and unending "luminous darkness." We thus are on the way toward developing new human capacities.

~

~

Heartfulness, wondrously, never results in becoming "spacey." Quite the opposite — a very different sense of being grounded occurs, the grounding of being completely "here," felt from within.

This second sphere of heart awareness — heart-presence with others — also intensifies the confidence of feeling within our very Being, that is, the sense of "completeness," though we are far from "completed." We experience embodied heart-soul-spirit qualities of presence among all of the presences of the world. We are not actually within the world when experiencing ourselves only as independent from all that we are within. Heartfulness helps us experience how we are a radiance of particularity — aware, in body, and able to feel an unbounded sense of embodiment. If heartfulness of relating is imagined as only a matter of extending individual heart awareness toward another person, we inevitably fall back into a kind of contrived heartfulness, and the process tends toward forming sentimentalized ego presence.

~

～

All human beings exist as heart-presences. It happens the moment we emerge from the womb, probably before. The astounding, incomparable joy in seeing a newborn child perhaps goes beyond the newborn being "our child," or that of someone close to us. A birth reveals the human being as heart-presence, and we feel those qualities within us too, for heartfulness activates in such moments. From that moment on, though, covering and layering occurs, until in this civilization, we no longer see nor feel we are within a heart-presence, except in exceptional times of intimacy that cannot be sustained. We see a human being "over there," in front of us, perhaps talking, and maybe we are trying to understand each other, or become even closer, not able to notice that as far as the heart is concerned, this distance does not exist.

This image of seeing another person as if truly seeing a person for the first time, like a newborn child, has to be retrieved, not naively, but with the same kind of care that was involved in developing individual heart awareness.

～

Heart-Presence With Another Person

To begin a prayer/practice that initiates heart-relating as an ongoing way of being present with others, ask someone you know to simply sit with you for a little while.

With your eyes closed, enter the Sealing prayer/practice as developed earlier. (Alternately, do the four key prayer/practices in full.) Then, open your eyes and simply be within your heart with the other person. Without speaking, remain within the felt sense of heartfulness with the other person, until you feel it fade.

From the moment our eyes open, we find ourselves within the sensory world and a new unfolding of heart-presence now begins. This second sphere of heartfulness — the initial sphere of sustained "world-heartfulness" — constitutes a reversal from what we have been doing. The immediate question becomes how to sustain and maintain a sense of the subtlety of heart, in the midst of the strength of sensation. A tendency to fall into heart-sentiment comes forth . . . but if this occurs, we have left heart-presence for emotion.

Notice first what happens to your sensing and perceiving of the other person. How is it different, arising from the place of the heart, than our usual way of being with another person? Then, you might also want to ask the other person to describe what he or she experienced in this quiet sitting.

Entering this sphere of heartfulness requires us to be able to stay within a more relaxed sensory perceptual presence with another person, a loosening of our object-oriented perceiving. Notice a permeation and surround of radiance while perceiving the other person with heart-connected noticing. Perceiving itself now feels imbued with heartfulness. The heartfulness aspect only occurs as long as we feel, simultaneously, heart and other. The kind of forgetful presence of someone "already there" dims, and the creating of presence, in this moment, intensifies perceiving with its inherent but usually unnoticed aura of "oneness" with who we are with.

～

MUTUAL HEART-PRESENCE

A second heartfulness prayer/practice of relating asks that you are able to be with another person, in the Silence, for a short time, and that together you are going to experience mutual heart-presence.

Start with the Heart Alignment, the Silence, Heart-Awareness — or enter into the Sealing prayer/practice. As you now face the person from within heartfulness, place your visual attention at a specific place, such as a button on the shirt of the other person, something innocuous; we are not engaged in mutual "gazing," we do not seem, nor do we "try" to make something happen. As sensory focus centers on a particular place, at the same time, allow your vision to peripherally extend beyond the bodily form of the other person. Let your vision be simultaneously focused at the one place, while diffusely extending even beyond the person. At first, this kind of sensation may seem odd, and even be a kind of strain. During this prayer/ practice, for the time being, both individuals remain silent.

Within a few minutes, in becoming accustomed to this "focus-diffuse" sensing, an utterly innocent "merging" with the other person occurs, as if the space between you can be felt. When you feel this moment of the subtlety of unity, close your eyes and allow the feeling presence of the other person to continue. (Before beginning this prayer/practice, you might want to tell the other person of this process and invite the other person to close her/his eyes when you close yours, and just be present.)

It is as if you and the other person are being held within an embrace of intimacy, an intimacy unlike any felt before. No entanglement whatsoever occurs. Both you and the other person remain completely free, and in fact, what happens in meeting in this way concerns the initial waking-up within our bodily-emotional freedom. Instead of the scary and entirely premature and inappropriate possibility of emotional entanglement that immediately makes one want to pull away, we experience the full and true holiness that is this person. We do so through the center of the true holiness of our own Being. We awaken to and within our and the other's personhood. We experience, directly, sensorily, the other-as-person, through the heart as medium of our personhood.

Now, ask the other person what was experienced. You might even go through the process of helping the other person enter heartfulness, and do the prayer/practice again. This time, you are sitting quietly with the other person while that person is with you in heartfulness.

~

When we meet another person in this kind of encounter, we do not want it to stop. We wish it would go on forever, as the presence of Reverence now emerges. It has been here all along, but we only begin to sense it now as a new way of bodily, heart, presence. We do not try to make this happen or contrive it happening in any way. An actual Being of Reverence seems to come and be present whenever we are within heartfulness with another person.

Reverence also seems a quite passive word. However, it has its own activity; feeling now touches into action, for the two, heartfulness and action, co-exist. Reverence is "to revere," an act, a doing of the receptive will. We find ourselves holding the other person with awe and honor. Nothing exterior imposed a "will" to do so. Reverence is the exact, right word for what occurs, for it entails neither worship nor veneration, but rather, it is as if noticing for the first time the visibility of the other person as a radiance.

~

⁓

Encountering another person through heartfulness initiates us into a new kind of action, alluded to earlier — "non-doing-doing." Meeting another in this way involves the will of the heart. Here, much more than with individual heartfulness, we can experience "will-reversal." Will forces begin transforming from willfulness to *willingness*. Any agendas we have, conscious or unconscious, in being with another person, begin to dissolve. These agendas, such as wanting simply to be with another person as an escape from loneliness, or a need to be liked, or wanting to demonstrate our power over another . . . these melt away, even while we might still have a necessary relation with another person that involves "getting something done." While this habitual, necessary action goes on, heartfulness becomes the truer reason of our relating. A transformation of will begins.

⁓

~

Will, to the extent we can be aware of it at all through its reflection into mental presence, occurs as an impulse, turned into a thought, that we then seek to bring about in action — a hefty sequence, for sure, and one taking place almost entirely unconsciously. Will functions without our having any sense of how it happens. For example, the typing of these words, as it happens, can happen only through the direct action of the will, felt within the fibers of the nerves and muscles of the hand. Conceptual knowing does not enter — except as a lagging kind of mental conception of what happens, or as a conceptual knowing of what I am about to do in approaching the keyboard. The actual typing, though, occurs through the action of the will, which remains outside our available consciousness, functioning wholly bodily. We use this mental conception to start it happening again — "I am now going to write," which we take to be will.

Will itself *acts*, rather than thinking first and then putting the thinking into action. The intervention of thinking keeps us from spontaneity and creative action. A good football player reveals something very close to pure will. Pure will can be characterized as "explosive," happening immediately, forcefully, without a moment's hesitation. A stockbroker can do the same thing. It seems to start with a mental notion of, "I'm going to sell $50,000 of stock today." The rest reveals the same kind of "explosive" will forces, a kind of back and forth between mind and will.

～

～

Heartful presence with another excludes any of the usual will qualities described. But we are doing something; this shall become even more evident as this will-presence of the heart develops further. The usual distinction between "being and doing," one that many spiritual paths fondly invoke, seems quite illusory, and almost certainly results in the "held back" will erupting in unusual ways.

We cannot really hold back will. Will reveals the most basic embodiment of spirit. If we are embodied we are within will; it's as if it exists within the fibers of the nerves and muscles. It is much more likely that the "being-doing" distinction has not carefully noticed what actually happens in "being" — which is will as completely receptive, and thus "active" in an entirely new way.

～

—

Receptive will forms the very basis, the given foundation for contemplative heart action. The best region to first notice the manner in which receptive will acts, occurs with heart-presence with another person. We do not simply go silent and into "being" with another person, and when that finishes, then get back to the action of the will where things can "really happen." Unless will itself can be felt in its completeness, heartfulness remain as one of those ways of "being," and ineffective as a world force. With heartful encounters, I become you; you become me, with awareness. We are, as spiritual human beings, always brothers and sisters. Boundaries, though, are never violated, because this kind of unified presence with another person takes place beyond the spheres of desire, want, need, agenda, and certainly, thinking.

—

With the receptive will of the heart, a sequence of "cause-effect," which is the usual way we determine how something happens in the world, no longer holds. Presence with another person from within heartfulness instantaneously also enters into the world; something actually happens — an action, a receptive action, has taken place. How do we know that something has happened in the world if we cannot say something like, "Yes, I was within heartfulness with another person and as a result this person was much kinder and present with me. The cause of this change in the other person was what I did." Another person does not register heartfulness with the mind and then respond accordingly. A causal sequence does not occur; rather, a mutual event happens. It may help our noticing if the other person has become bodily sensitive to heart, but regardless of whether or not this happens, the event of heartfulness happens, and it is always a mutual event.

There are further means of verifying that heartfulness enters into the world instantaneously, even if it visibly shows up later. Noticing the action within the world also requires relaxed receptivity, rather than looking for a result as if we were expecting an effect, which easily turns into using heartfulness to try to achieve something for ourselves.

Heartful presence with another reveals itself, not in what the other person does or does not do in relation to the encounter. Maybe only later, much later, something shows up in the world and we realize that it is related to the event of being within heart-presence with a particular person. The circumstances in which this kind of "doing" can occur will be presented, but heart-listening has to be able to be noticed first.

⁓

Speaking With Another Person
Within Heart-Presence

A third prayer/practice within this sphere of our being with others concerns noticing how speaking with someone changes radically from within heartfulness.

Earlier, we introduced the sense of language as gestural power. Language always already exits. Language is a gift, just as life, death, and birth are gifts. Language exists before we speak. We have to meet language. Our usual way of being with language works completely habitually; it seems that we just speak, and have learned to do so. Experiencing the autonomous power of the word when gestured through the heart belies habitual language use.

From within the heart, when we gesture words, the word can be felt as an actual presence, and it recedes when we are quiet. Only from the place of ego consciousness do we think that we originate language; in truth, we only speak it, but to do so, it must be present. Such presence can be felt when we speak from within heartfulness. The presence of language does not refer to meaning, but to doing. Language "does" before it means. Poetry, for example, consists of this wondrous quality of language as power — and particularly as receptive power. Poetry both "does" and "feels present," and the doing registers receptively when we read it. We may be "blown away" with beauty, but it actually feels much more like being blown "into" by beauty, such is the intimate power of language gesture.

Ask your friend if she or he will enter the place of the heart with you again. Then indicate that this time what you are both going to try and do is to speak aloud with each other while being consciously focused within the heart. This means that while one person is speaking, the other person remains fully within heart-presence while listening; the same thing occurs when there is the switching of who is talking and who is listening. The first time doing this, it is helpful to choose something to speak about. Suggest, for example, that you speak together about what brings you joy.

This prayer/practice typically result in feeling more intimate with the other person than we have ever felt with anyone. The intimacy does not occur emotionally, as a reaction to being truly noticed and recognized. Rather, intimacy is the character of mutual heart-presence, where we both, for a time, forget our ego-centeredness.

⁓

CONTEMPLATIVE
HEART-LISTENING

~

We live within a "pronouncement civilization." Little is said or written concerning the receiving side of addressing others, though techniques do exist. Far less attention goes toward addressing the world and Earth in such a way that we begin to feel in ongoing conversational relation with what so intimately surrounds us.

~

—

A wholly pronouncement-oriented civilization promotes overly-confident intellectuality, emotion, and the imposition of will. Opinions go back and forth between people, one person pouring forth their pronouncements of intellect and opinions, while the other awaits a turn — not to respond, but to do the same thing to the other person. If we learn to wait politely or to mirror back to others what they just said, then we imagine we have learned some techniques of listening. Earth seems to have nothing inherent to do with what we do or how we act.

—

—

Developing the heart capacity to speak from within the primordial listening of Earth and Cosmos differs immensely from a listening technique. Such listening implies a different cosmology than that which we currently live within. If we assume that creation began with a "big bang," that view becomes the template of all that happens. "Big Bang" theory results in an explosive world; it is enacted within the explosive impulsiveness of willfulness, and a reliance on deriving energy from internal combustion, bullets, guns, rockets. It fills our streets and minds with violence, fear, and terror. The cosmology itself becomes the archetypal image we live by. We shall here stretch that cosmology for all it is worth, finding ourselves moved outside of it, and only further on speak more of the Cosmology of Rhythm, where we are tending.

—

Earth, together with Her expression as Nature, forms the greatest of all vessels of true Silence, and thus of true listening. Earth and Nature also speak, but in such a manner that the Silence always exists in the foreground. This right-order reverses what we know as speaking and listening, where speaking always comes to the foreground while the creative ground of the Silence disappears altogether. We live primordially within the rhythms of the Silence and revelation, but live civiizationally with precedence given to who can make the loudest pronouncements. In this time, the noise tends toward science and technology, accompanied by greed and pervasive commodification.

As I listen, for example, to the rustling of the leaves of the trees outside my door, the rhythm of the breeze, the soft sounds, and the delicate movement of the branches pull me into the Silence. It takes very little attention to listen. Right here, we have before us the demonstration of a very different kind of cosmology than the one we have come to adhere to. It is not at all that Nature speaks to us, we listen, and then respond, even if that response is no more than a kind of sigh of joy. Thinking of listening in this way puts us right back in the "pronouncement" universe. We have not really listened. We misuse the Silence of the world and Earth when the most we take in and feel of primordial Being consists of moments of refreshment.

—

~

We can be present with Nature in a primordial act of listening because Nature herself listens! The world of matter, the world that matters, listens. This kind of listening constitutes the heart of Earth. Many feel this, but cannot articulate it well in the dominant language of science and technology, which thus invents terms like "ecology."

The Greek word *physis,* from which we receive the words "physics" and "physical," originally meant "a process of a-rising, of emerging from the hidden" — emerging every moment — from within the Silence. This arising of things from the Silence occurs as a Whole, a unity. It is a Whole-coming-into-being. Thus, when you enter into the Silence, you feel the active presence of receptive Wholeness. The Silence does not divide into parts.

~

~

When we listen, truly listen to someone, we are abiding within our place as Earthly beings, and we do something very unusual. We hear, not the word, but rather, *through* the word we hear the particularity of the Silence as it configures itself to the moment. In order to listen, which has little to do with the quiet we are in while someone speaks, something else has to go on — what we hear as known content has to every moment be sacrificed, given away, forgotten as content, in order to hear the Silence addressing us.

~

Heart-Listening Within Nature

Take a walk. Begin to listen while being within the Silence and heart-presence. Seeing, walking, touching, hearing, smelling, being within the plethora of sensing and being within the heart — all are modes of listening with Nature. Attempt to listen to the deep Silence of the physical world — not the given physical world as you typically notice it. Notice how the Silence is very different as you stand and simply notice, from within heart-presence, a tree, and then a boulder, or a plant, moving water, a breeze, or anything else of Nature. Each presence emerges from the Silence as a particular expressing of the Silence. Even each particular thing — one tree, and next to it another tree of the same kind, speak the Silence very individually.

～

Feeling Earth as living presence forms the very ground of listening; She is the "third" who exits between any two in true conversation, holding us in conversations of Wholeness while subverting the prevalence of abstracting, by beckoning us into to the ongoing instances of the reconfiguring of Wholeness into moments of particularity.

We do not merely stand "on" the Earth, we are of the substance of Earth, and thus listening resounds Earth's presence through individual body-presence. The matter of body is itself a reconfiguration of Earth into the particularity not of just "body," but "this bodying" that "I am."

～

～

When someone speaks and we listen, not just with our ears but with the whole of our being centered in the heart, the speaking can be felt bodily. We usually hear through our ears and listen with our head. Now, we can begin to feel a subtle bodily resonance. This resonance is its own way of knowing, something essentially wordless and thus pre-cognitive. Gradually, this resonance can be brought into harmony with the content we are hearing, and we then hear the person in his or her variation as aspects of Earth presence. If you remember what it is like listening to someone speak when there is a strong presence of love between you, this Whole-listening intensifies that kind of feeling beyond the merely personal. The kind of listening we are drawing attention to here does not have the reactive, emotional component that presents with feelings of love. Intimate heart-listening, in unity with Earth presence, frees itself of the egotistical component often present with the bloom of love, and is always new and mature at the same moment.

～

Heart-Listening With Earth

With contemplative-spiritual listening we are asked to be aware of staying in body, to be present with the felt resonance of the speaking. Some practice helps to both become aware of what it is like to "descend" from the head to the heart in listening, and to feel currents spreading through the body.

Make a descent into the soul-body by shifting attention that is habitually located in the region of the head to the region of the heart. Notice that you sense the Silence, and through the Silence, sense the Earthly soul/spirit particularity of where you stand or sit. Then, while attention can be felt in the heart, simultaneously place attention in the region of the feet. When you speak with someone — in an instant, but with felt body-ness — re-enact this descent.

～

If I am sitting on the porch watching the trees — well, that is all the mind registers: trees, and perhaps an emotional response of relief from anxiousness for a moment, or a sigh of letting go for a moment. Mental registering of sensation occurs so strongly that the "silent speaking" of the trees, while still present, is severely dimmed. When we shift attention to the heart and feet, sense the world, and feel the body resonance, then we see something like: the rhythmic swaying of a tall tree in the background while those closer are like guardian sentinels of the playful rhythms of what is going on behind them. The sunlight touches a portion of the trees as the shadows reach back and engulf the leaves behind, darkening them into a sense of mystery. Through the thickness of the swaying and the quiet greening, the soft, light blue above shows through, revealing a different reality, a far-ness that is invited into the play of the rhythm, and indeed, feels as if forming the very source of the swaying green movement.

～

—

Such listening lingers on bodily, long after the experience. We feel altered by the experience of allowing Earth to penetrate us. The bodily-felt lingering inaugurates a process of transformation. When listening in this same manner with another person, listening through the heart of the Silence, feeling the currents of Earth, full presence with another person as embodied spiritual Earth-human — mutual transforming occurs.

—

HEART-LISTENING WITH
HEART-EARTH-ANOTHER PERSON

Listening does not involve going out-of-body as cognitive hearing does, but rather falling into the joy of sensing, in very particular ways. We enter into the vibratory force of another through the vibratory field of our own body. It is like being in a musical field, having rhythm, tone, and octave. And, while one is within this I-Earth-Thou field, something else goes on — we are held in oneness with the Spiritual Earth. Earth feels, in her own ways, this kind of conversing; She not only participates in the conversations, She transforms too. Unless this kind of intimate participation with others occurs, Earth remains perceived as simply the "stage" upon which life exists.

Such a radical way of considering listening needs to be tested.

Sit with a friend within the Silence of the heart. Notice the tonality that you, together, create, through noticing your body-presence while sensing Earth-presence. Speak with each other, trying to speak the qualities of being together in this way without losing the felt sense of the tonality. Avoid interpreting what you think body experiences. Experience the speaking of the other in its gestural manifestation. Do not be concerned about understanding each other, for that will produce a shifting into cognition.

—

A very simple practice, for sure, a powerful prayer/practice that has to be repeated, probably over a long period of time in order to override habitual cognitive presence with others, and ease the anxiety of releasing any agendas — particularly the agenda of making sure you understand and speak in ways that assure the other person understands. Understanding does not leave. It trails on behind the truth of heart-body presence, now consciously occurring.

Listening becomes an active form of wordless inner communion with others, through which we can be present to the arising of the new octave of Earthly soul/spirit presence of the other person and feel ourselves similarly transforming, through the presence of a subtle, inaudible, but felt "hum" of the heart. The emerging new self has to be called out through the listening process. Listening as midwifery.

—

Putting understanding ahead of listening interferes with the listening. To maintain our listening means maintaining a continuous sense of not-understanding, an open waiting. *To try and make the other person clarify what I do not understand as listener shuts down the listening.* The access to the inner being of the other person is through the not-understood. To try and make the person clarify the not-understood so that I can understand means that I am making the person speak according to what I already know, and shuts down transformation into "Earth-listeners."

LISTENING FOR THE EMERGING WORD

Maintaining listening to what is not understood deepens the presence of the Silence within the speaking, even when the activity of speaking goes on. We become more able to be present with absolute inner Silence. We learn to hold someone in our "aural gaze," just as when we gaze into the eyes of a beloved. We know when we are listening when the felt-quality of loving can be heard through the expanding Silence.

Engage with a prayer/practice of speaking together with someone while maintaining the Silence, not only while listening to the other person, but within your own speaking.

Notice the tendency of speaking to "get ahead of itself." When we begin to feel we are waiting to say something we want to say, let attention return more deeply into the Silence. Listen inwardly for the emerging creation of what wants to speak, rather than what we want to speak.

Feel the bodily field and feel how what the other person says lives within us, bodily, rather than understood mentally. Allow words to come with their own rhythm and timing, which will occur, quite naturally, much slower than a mental pace.

~

Listening involves giving someone our attention. That is a remarkable gift, the gift of our spirit-being. Giving someone attention is an act, a doing very different than paying attention to what the other person says. When we simply "pay attention," we retain attention, focusing it on ourselves, and seem to give a little part of it, as if stingily handing out money. Typically, when we pay attention, we do not utilize much attention at all. Rather, we temporarily, for a moment, restrain our ego-presence, holding it back, waiting to release it once again. True attention is not like that.

~

～

Attention is whole. It cannot be divided into parts, holding on to one part, giving another part away. Giving attention in listening holds someone within the most intimate aspect of our being, our spirit — not abstractly spiritual, but Earthly-spiritual. We strongly feel that we are holding the other person and at the same time feel the embrace of Earth. The capacity of Earth-heart-listening forms a new contemplative/practical spiritual path.

Everything changes into presence with radical receptivity. Dedication to this mode of listening involves stilling the various levels of our being — the intellectual, the desire, the psychological, and the ego dimensions. We do not do the stilling, but gradually come to be able to rest within Stillness.

～

Finding the Heart Space of Reverent Waiting

The prayer/practice is simple: we enter the Silence, and heart-presence, and then gradually we find ourselves in the "waiting space." This space is real, filled with peacefulness that is whole, round, interior, fluid; and while waiting, "waiting for something to happen" does not take over. Gradually, we become able to be in this space with another person, even while talking, certainly while listening.

Go into the Silence and place attention in the center of the heart. Then, make an image, seeing yourself inwardly, lying on your back, floating on a clear, calm, lake.

Be within this image — go into it. There will come a moment when you actually feel that you are floating on a clear, calm lake. The body will be floating there. As long as you are present within this sensation of floating on the lake, your mind will be clear and not occupied with thinking. You have given consciousness something "to do" that is not thinking. You will be able to notice, "out of the corner of your consciousness" as you are floating on the clear, calm lake, the complete relaxation of the body — and also what the "empty mind, full-heart" feels like. Once we bodily experience this "waiting space," it becomes ever easier to find when with others.

＿

In the hearing phase of listening, we maintain listening by the continuous sense of "not-understanding"; being within the quietness of mind and quietness of vital, emotional being, within the "waiting space." Being within such empty-fullness, within body, feeling Earth's waiting listening, far from passivity, exercises the power of receptivity. This receptive force, felt by the one speaking as welcoming, and like a magnetic current, draws what is unknown by the speaker into speaking. Then, a turning point of listening occurs. We do not just respond to what we have heard in listening; to do so breaks the contemplative tone of listening and we find ourselves thrown back into usual conversation.

＿

～

When someone speaking stops, an inward gathering of the spirit/soul essence of what was spoken occurs within the heart-earth unity. We can feel that gathering; it feels something like holding our breath, with ease, underwater, though here it is the depth of the heart. If we try to directly speak to the one who has spoken, it will be felt as an interpretation, or as a kind of pronouncement.

～

—

We feel the response being born! We may experience speaking in faltering fashion, full of pauses, in sentences not quite polished, certainly not at all pre-thought. A feeling of imperfection indicates being within the "coming-to-be" of a response. To get a sense of what this kind of response may be like, let responding to someone slow down, remain within the Silence and within the heart. Practice is required because we live in the civilization of products, and language has become a product, ready at hand, already completed, to be used to try and make something happen in predictable ways. The language of true spiritual conversation carries with it the whole realm of possibility contained within the Silence of the heart, now configured as this particular moment with another person.

—

The spiritual way of conversation engages two or more people in mutual heart initiation, awakening the capacity to be present, together, with the spiritual Earth, here, in-body, here, in-world, here, as Earthly beings. Spiritual initiation has always been understood as the result of individual meditative or contemplative practice, done alone, or alongside the presence of others, but not with others. The spiritual-Earth exists, has always existed as the invisible but real presence, both of the heart of the cosmos, and between ourselves and others. Awakening occurs in the moment of the birthing of speech, within the act of listening.

~

Psychotherapy might seem to also consist of the kind of listening and speaking described here. Is there a difference between "psychological listening" and spiritual, contemplative listening? Are we taking psychotherapeutic method out of the office into the street? Typically in a psychological approach, the listener hears absence, void, and thus longing, need, desire, want, seeking. When we listen in terms of lack, in terms of someone trying to find an answer to something missing within themselves, then we are engaged in psychological listening. In a spiritual approach to listening, overwhelming Wholeness always resounds. Nothing in the nature of lack or absence is noticed, not in those initiatory moments. Everything is already here and present, and the work is completely oriented toward developing the inner capacity of hearing the fullness of the present.

Is it necessary for both people in conversation to be aware of entering a prayer/practice? No. The inner essence of everyone awaits this chance, this possibility of spiritual awakening that can occur only through the heart-presence of another person, now united with us.

~

The prayer/practices presented around and fostering such awakening might produce the impression that heartful presence together always happens with sweetness and tender care. Such caring, though, can also occur in the most difficult kinds of conversations and relating, those filled with conflict. In fact, conflict with someone may present the strongest possibility of spiritual listening. Such a possibility usually goes by unnoticed because of the fear that accompanies conflict, fear resulting in a contraction of soul-body-heart-earth presence. The realm of the "between" easily obscures, and we feel abandoned by any sort of connecting presence, isolated, and unable to realize that when we try to speak out of such isolation with another person, we are essentially engaged in an unconscious monologue with ourselves.

Heart-Listening Within Conflict

Trying to listen in the midst of conflict put us in a situation of great tension, the tension of opposites, and this tension produces its own "between" field, a strong field of oscillation. If the oscillation itself can be felt, then one or both people will not fall into their isolated, separate demands that become projectiles of defensiveness. Oscillating between two isolated presences can begin to dissolve into mutual vibratory presence. When we have developed depth in heartfulness, enough *cour-age* lives within us consciously to be able to listen to the oscillation itself. The urge to win the fight diminishes. Entering into the midst of the oscillating field can be hastened with a simple practice/technique:

When conflict with someone begins:

l. Take a breath: Inhale and identify within you what is upsetting you.

2. Let go of it as you exhale.

3. Second breath: Inhale and feel the Silence at the center of your being.

4. Exhale.

5. Third breath: Inhale and ask yourself inwardly "What's next?" Listen.
   Exhale and notice what emerges.

Much can happen with this small practice; it relocates conflict from the sphere of inevitable painfulness to an important aspect of heartful listening.

~

Beyond technique, however, lies the question of the spiritual importance of conflict — how to avoid psychologizing conflict and instead take the situation of conflict into the practice of creative listening, not to try and resolve conflicts or learn how to get along better with someone. If, in a given situation, the conflict takes over, then it is more like a contemplation that did not go so well rather than an emotional disaster.

~

~

In order to follow the contemplative path of listening in a situation of conflict, returning to the particularity of the configuring of the Silence into this tense moment becomes the central practice. When speaking is kept very specific, without any generalizations whatsoever, the false beings of conflict have no place to play. The beings of conflict fool us into thinking that what we say is indeed the truth and the other person does not see the truth. But conflict does not have anything to do with truth; it does have to do with the invitation to develop an unattached speaking of what one feels is happening.

~

~

This requirement forms a main manner in which conflict can become a situation for the spiritual practice of listening. Listening cannot occur when abstractions or generalizations or sentiments or notions taken from somewhere else, or clichés, or truisms enter. Abstract reactions fire up the conflict, so these hindrances show up very clearly.

~

~

Volatile situations are charged with wanting to win. With a backdrop of heartfulness one gets a chance to see that "attack mentality" within oneself as an intensification of an emotional tone that usurps soul's own intensity, or sparking fire, so that intensity cannot, instead, enter into heartfulness. Heartful listening has no intention other than the listening itself. Everything within listening carries its own inherent meaning. Volatile emotion introduces an agenda, the agenda of force.

~

～

What is the spiritual purpose of conflict? This is the kind of question appropriate to the spirituality of listening. Here, with heart-listening, we enter into the question that takes the whole phenomenon of conflict out of the realm of emotion and out of the realm of psychological difficulties, and even out of the realm of viewing conflict as something gone wrong.

Conflict provides the opportunity to see all that interferes with listening, but also brings the opportunity to listen through the difficulties rather than living in a emotional/psychological fantasy that they have to be gotten rid of, and only then can true listening happen.

～

~

Emotion does not hinder heartfulness — the egotizing of emotion does. The practice above constitutes only a beginning of contemplative work to release emotion from the egotistic use of emotion, revealing a very different way to be with emotion as the felt announcing of the quickening of body in preparation for spiritual listening, for the arrival of what we don't know, rather than perpetuating what we already do know that has begun to calcify.

~

Transforming Emotional Reaction into Heartful Emotion

The word "e-motion" carries the connotation that emotion concerns the motion or movement of the soul — that is, emotion constitutes the very moment, the very instant of the transforming of pure spiritual presence announcing itself into the motion of the fabric of time, the bodying-forth of spirit into the substance and action of life. All life, then, is emotion, but not emotional reaction. Emotional reaction stops the movement of spirit into the substance of life, and thus emotionality keeps us stuck, often permanently.

Begin with writing a narrative of an emotional memory — what occurred, what the emotion is like, what was the outcome.

As you read the story, notice how the egotizing of emotion relies a great deal on the "skimming" of a memory — that is, omitting important but consciously available details of the memory. So, the second step, after writing the emotional memory-narrative, is to go back, enter the presence of the memory from the place of the Silence and the region of the heart, feeling the embrace of Earth, and notice where absent details begin to be available. Make notes of these details, which is the first "acknowledgement" of the holiness of the memory itself — the recognition that there is more to what occurred than the ego is wanting us to see.

In the "expanding" memory — that is, as the memory frees from the egotizing reactionary process — the sense of the "memory" as not really a memory at all, but an imaginal event that is happening, now emerges. As you feel the event happening now, however, you do not see yourself as the center of the emotion, as in the narration memory. When we are within an emotional event, we do not see ourselves, we are an aspect of a whole unfolding world — of another, or others, the surroundings, the light, the tonality of the moment, the sense of time. With the egotizing of the emotion, which occurs immediately, almost spontaneously, we *become the center and the all. The emotion as flow gets covered and captured by ego to keep the memory stuck in repetitiveness, rather than emotion as the very force of spirit in life.*

Repeat the emotion-breathing practice, given earlier, with this purified imagination of the event. Notice being closer with the presence of the emotion, and to the spiritual emotion-body. From within the Silence and the heart, now re-live the emotion-event — saying what you said, saying what you were thinking, feeling the same feeling, gesturing with your body, letting the event "act" . . . again, however, doing so from within the Silence and being within the heart — giving the holy space necessary.

Heartful Action

~

Contemplating heartful action takes us into relatively unknown places of soul and spirit, the spiritual/soul realms of the will — that is, very deep into body-awareness, to the very edge of where awareness can go.

We seem to understand what it means to act; we do so all of the time, and we may try to do so in ways that are of service. Action with heart awareness, and in unity with the world, though, requires special attentiveness that breaks our habitual consciousness of the causality of act and consequence.

Heartful action entails more than doing something in the world — it requires doing so *while* being aware within heart's "doing" as presence with the physical world, the soul worlds, and the spiritual worlds all at once, from within conscious heart-presence.

~

~

Heartful action and its world consequences cannot be noticed the way we usually causally connect action and result. The separation we are accustomed to — of act followed by consequence in linear time — does not occur with this kind of action. We enter a different current of time, the time of the heart, the fourth dimension, through which we notice the coherence of time and space. But *where and how* heartful action reveals itself in the world bears little relation to the literal character of the act and any expected consequences. We cannot directly see what happens in the world within the linear time of the act.

~

When we do some self-oriented act, we have the capacity to be aware of the focus, "I am doing this act for myself." When we seem to be engaged in doing something for others, or for some consequence in the world, we seem not so ego-aware, and ego actually is open to having free reign, though in disguised ways, primarily power. Without developing inner awareness, our actions, in one way or another, revolve around serving ourselves, if not directly, then indirectly. We live in a time of hyper self-consciousness, one which invades all awareness, for it does not segment itself into just one region. This reality serves as the necessary starting place for developing the capacities of heartful action.

—

The word "ego," and its cohort "self" are words — like body, or soul, or spirit, or even heart — that easily become abstractions, and begin to mean just about anything. Throughout this writing, any use of the term "ego" intends to convey a sense of the capacity for the immediate knowing of "otherness," and each specific "otherness" as isolated and separate; this "otherness" even subsumes the intimacy of our own being, reduced to only a small aspect of the fullness of who we are as human. We nonetheless identify with this power-awareness. While "ego" knows through separation, its acts are always for the sake of ego itself, even if what we do seems to be for the sake of others. Our "self-interest" horns its way in, even in the most altruistic of actions.

—

—

Such characterizing of ego serves as a kind of guide we need in considering heartful action, but we need even something more — a kind of inner awareness of ego that is other than ego-awareness. A slippery matter, but necessary if we are not to confuse heartful action with ego-action, or dissolve into a kind of blissful oblivion when within heartfulness.

What we speak of as "I" quite automatically serves as the reference, unknown of course, to egotism, where ego's "knowing" is of ego alone. When we speak of "I" — for example, in saying something like, "I want to be helpful to the world" — this "I" automatically acts self-referentially for itself. In this example, while "I" seem to be oriented toward others, such an orientation, for the "ego-I," is an impossibility.

—

～

However, a deeper and much more spiritual sense of "I," where "I" speaks the reality of the most unknowable aspect of being, the center, actually equivalent and perhaps the same as heart awareness, does exist. The spiritual sense of "I" only persists within a sustained felt quality of a creating of every moment, with and in unity with whatever awareness may be present at a particular moment. The "I" here, then, does something that our usual sense of "I" cannot — it exists only in the moment, invisibly, in unity with what we are aware of, a particularizing of spirit with each and every person. This particularizing cannot be separated from heart or from the harmony of incarnating as body-substance each and every moment.

～

—

We can meet the usual "ego" awareness through heart-presence, and doing so immediately relativizes this usual awareness so that we become able to curtail its tendency to take over the world.

We find an entry into heartful action by actually meeting Who our usual ego-I looks like and feels like. Ego is not the individual you see in the mirror, nor you as you imagine yourself to be, or who others address when speaking with you, so we cannot meet "ego" by any usual means, for it is a medium of presence, not a thing. And ego is also not that very deep and subtle and light center of the heart of your being, you as "spiritual-I," which can be known only from within the heart.

—

MEETING EGO

We can indirectly meet ego through an act of imagining, which awakens an awareness — "Oh, this is what ego is like." A prayer/practice for meeting ego has the qualification that we can sense that the ego we meet is not a "literal" ego, for literalizing belongs to the very character of ego itself. Ego takes each separated awareness in a totally literal way — what is, is. No more, and no less. Ego does not include and cannot incorporate the capacity of imagining, for imagining is a soul capacity.

In order to meet "ego," then, we do so through a prayer/practice engaging the capacity of imagination, which allows us relief from the suffocation of literalism.

We begin with the Heart Alignment, and then allow attentiveness to appear within the interior of the heart. Then we enter the Silence and into Pure Body-Awareness and Heart-Awareness:

Imagine the presence of a being, who looks just like you, sitting with his/her back to your back, the backs touching each other. This being is of a subtle nature, so don't literalize the picture. It is both a felt sense of you, and you can picture the being as looking like you. The presence of this figure constitutes a variation of your individual spirit, the variation that can and does forget itself as a spiritual being, and instead tries to make its way through life on its own. We begin to get the sense of ego acting as if it were independent of the spiritual and soul realms.

Sit quietly, in the Silence. Then, let this presence glide like a breath through your body, touching every cell as it is moving from the back to the front. Let it move through you and then "float" in front of you. Look this presence in the eye (it will not be literally seen, much more felt) and admit its presence into the felt heart-field — the body-sensitivity that extends beyond the physical body. Be aware of the qualities, gestures, and features of this Being, no matter how difficult they might be. Let this being say what it wants to say to you. Hear it speak, though the hearing occurs within you, inaudibly, and may be more a feeling-sense than verbal. Let it tell you who it is and what it wants. Then, ask for the grace of change, that this presence does not dominate you unconsciously. Take time and let this unfold slowly. If you seem to be "making up" things, don't be concerned. Just notice.

After this is done, while you are sitting facing each other, feel the way in which both of you together form a rounded space with its midpoint between you.

Lead both figures — the ego and the immediate sense of your body — to this midpoint. Let them both lean slightly inward, into the vortex of the heart. Feel this movement. Be present to the qualities. The power of love that was previously frozen ego-awareness within begins feeling freed.

~

Having met "ego," let us now meet ourselves as "spiritual-I," the center of heartfulness.

Being able to do this prayer/practice, like all the prayer/practices, requires forces of attentiveness that are free and therefore able to concentrate with this prayer/practice without distraction. But, "Who," not what. Who, are these forces of attentiveness? They too seem to be us. However, attention is not the same "I" as ego capacities.

~

Meeting the "I" of Heartfulness

Ego, who we just met, continually thwarts the capacity of free, unattached attentiveness needed to meet the "I." We become distracted, wandering into thoughts or fantasies when we try to concentrate on something of a wholly inner nature. We cannot exactly "meet" this "I," not as we have met the presence of ego. We have to invent a kind of fiction of the "I," and carry through with a prayer/practice with this fiction. Meeting ego, too, was a kind of fiction, but this one goes further. "I" does not exist except in its own creative act of coming-to-be, each moment. "I" does not become any kind of "form" because "I" constitutes the form-ing itself. The forming "I" does not exist independently of the forming of everything else, but rather participates in "all-forming." "I" individualizes "all-forming" as the configuration we know as "me," but it is not the "me" who I think I know.

"I" exists as tangible invisibility, particularized. "I" is "no-thing" and can be imagined as the inner sanctuary of who we each truly are — incarnate spiritual beings — so this practice has to be understood as an imaginal practice. It is not an illusion, not by any means, but rather it is as if we can meet "I" only at a juncture of being clothed by what we already know. It is possible, though, to feel a sense of "I" in its "trailing clouds of glory."

Make an inner image of your full being as an egg-shaped multi-colored mist of light extending outside, around, and through your physical body.

At the center of this mist is a tiny spark — your usual "I."

You — as "I Am" — has existence outside this egg. See it as a golden mist reaching down to your multi-colored being.

Sometimes it reaches the surface of your being; sometimes it withdraws into the universe.

See it as a flowing, continual movement, like gentle waves kissing the shore. Sometimes the sun glistens in this golden mist making it finer and lighter.

Sometimes the sunlit mist shines into your egg-shaped being as through a dark forest — engaging your small "I," that tiny spark at the center of your being.

The tiny spark starts to flicker within you, and grows, becoming one with the sunlit mist.

The "I Am" Mantras

To be inwardly, bodily-gesturally said, from the place of the central point of the heart:

This I Am is a body of Light
I Am a body of Light

This I Am is a body of Silence
I Am a body of Silence

This I Am is a body of Love
I Am a body of Love

~

These two practices — Meeting the "I" of Heartfulness, and The "I Am" Mantras — form essential aspects for entering into heartful, contemplative action. They are contemplative practices that need to be done with a regular rhythm, such as every other day at the same time, for a while, and then repeated periodically.

~

The French word for heart, *coeur*, enters the English language in the word *courage;* the "age" at the end of courage means "act." Thus, in its core, courage refers to the specific way heart spiritually functions — always. This *cour-age* differs from the heroic kind of action we usually associate with this word. We feel it with each beat of the heart. Heart's ongoing courageous action can be imagined as continual radiating "I-heart-forces," each moment conveying the essence of our being, our intentions, the tone of our actions — everything we are in action, into the world. We shape the world through the manner in which we receive the world into our hearts, and the world too shapes our very being and presence.

～

Rather than thinking of the ongoing interacting of heart and world in linear, causal terms, this reciprocal action might be imagined as mutual intermingling of receptivity, something like the kneading of dough, where the movement all occurs from within, and the kneading and the kneader are indistinguishable in time. An intimate conversation constantly goes on between heart and the heart of the world.

～

The mutual receptivity of heart action becomes sensorially and perceptibly noticeable only as it becomes perceptually "spread out" in the world. We do not sense-feel the relation of heart-action and its world-revealing as a cause-effect relation. The mutual receptivity becomes perceivable to us when we are within perceptual openness, primarily within the Silence of the Natural World. We also notice heart-action revealed through and in the actions of others. While possible, perceiving mutual heart-receptivity action within the built world remains more elusive.

The action of the heart becomes perceivable in moments of synchronicity in which we notice something in the world, and the heart immediately recognizes a world-occurrence as related to a receptive heart-act done with awareness.

～

Heart inherently acts within us and world simultaneously. Heart contemplation unites being with doing, occurs in the Silence, becomes sensed, noticed, perceived in the world through receptivity, synchronistically registering within heartfulness.

～

Heartful Action—Part I

Having seriously engaged the clearing and clarifying of ego, we then enter into a contemplation of the heart, holding an image there of a particular person, or an event, or a situation, or a condition going on somewhere in the world:

Begin with entering into Heart Alignment, the Silence, and Heart-Awareness.

Once within Heart-Awareness, inwardly, within the heart, make an image of who or what situation or event you are working with. The difficult part from here on is to be able to relinquish, completely, any desire or need to want to change the person or the event or situation. Hold this inner image without a "why." If any desire to do something can be felt, release this desire, while nonetheless holding the image with the qualities of whatever is happening — that is, if a person is suffering, or the situation is one of illness or tragedy or need, hold that image, making it as you would see the situation in the world, but without any desire or need to change it.

To hold this image within the heart with heart-tending, this central creating place of the heart, place you right hand over the place of your heart. When heart-sensitiveness and attentiveness has developed through engaging the prayer/practices sufficiently, this small gesture unites the will with the heart.

This unity is strongly felt as an overwhelming sense of receiving the heart-held image touching the palm of your hand and radiating back into the heart.

Gesture the name of the person or the event being held in this way. Feel the image being held come into the radiance of the heart, as if the heart-space becomes inner light. When felt, any notion of taking this creative act and using it for our own purposes becomes impossible without breaking the felt unity of the heart-will. Gradually, through this simple contemplation, become used to the qualities of this small place of the heart, the very center of contemplative action.

Heartful Action—Part II

The second aspect involves now noticing the action aspect of the contemplation within the world. It may not show up immediately, but should do so within three days of the first part of the contemplative action. It will appear as a synchronicity. That is, something will occur within the world, usually the Natural World, that is unmistakably the presence of what you engaged in contemplation, though in a very different form. The content of what we notice is not the primary quality that informs us of this extraordinary moment of perceiving being at-one with the contemplation. It will be a strong, subtle response of recognition. We feel a distinct quality of being "befriended" by a presence — this may be a bird, a stone, something in the landscape, a person, some object, or something occurring — felt, though, as an action. In itself, it will not seem related to the contemplation, but you will know, without question, that it is. This is the action-dimension of the contemplative action.

Contemplative action of heart, then, can be spoken of as a "non-doing-doing." Feeling acts mysteriously, and remains entirely "unspecialized." We do not know how the action will reveal itself. Whatever we are used to as service — helping, activism, or trying to get something to happen — are all very different than contemplative action. If we are involved in these kinds of practical actions, intending to be helpful, they can still be carried on as usual with all the difficulties and joys entailed — though now we are be much more aware of how power works, and that power needs to be curtailed through heartful action. We give up being able to quantify the effects of what we do and, even more, give up how we think the intentions of our actions make a difference.

What we do, its content, never constitutes heartful action; *how* we are with what we do determines whether our actions are heartful or not. Heartful actions always occur as if in "secret," though they are an open secret, of course. There is nothing "occult" in what we are suggesting here; only a kind of wisdom that cautiously understands that those around us are not likely to understand nor value contemplative action, nor even notice that it is the most profound of all action possible.

Examples:

One evening, as I sit in my office, holding in heart an image of a beloved person who died, nearly two years ago now . . . from within the heart I hear, inaudibly, the voice of this person. I, from the place of the heart, ask, "Are you here?" I feel his presence within the heart, but cannot sustain that presence, and notice the presence of doubt, just for a moment. The person then speaks again within my heart, saying: "Go outside." Again, I am brought into usual consciousness, and sit there for a few moments, swaying between doubt and awe. Then, without much conscious intent, I get up, walk downstairs and out the back door. It is a moment in which the world is at the edge of fall and winter, that moment when the line between light and dark thins. I look up and see a wondrous full moon. The moonshine is so strong — a great glow, reddish at the outer edges of the moon and radiating into silver-white into the surrounds, lights up the landscape. I am standing near the pond and can see the dark outlines of the surrounding trees. The night is filled with crisp wonder, but I do not feel anything more than the beautiful qualities of this moment.

Then, from nowhere, a flock of geese, many of them, fly in perfect order and harmony right in front of the moon, dark forms in perfect formation. I inwardly, within the heart, know, without an ounce of doubt anywhere, that this is the presence of my beloved friend. He is here. He teaches me the action of heartfulness.

Another instance:

The husband of a friend of mine walked away from home and disappeared. He has done this a number of times, so my friend, while disturbed, feels he will return. But return does not happen, not at 6 weeks, 8 weeks, 10 weeks. I enter into the kind of contemplation described. No intent to "find him" or hope that he will return, is present in the contemplation. The concern is completely for him and his presence, but nothing is attached to this concern. I allow the presence of an inner image of him and gesture his name. An overwhelming feeling of trust, but not "trust that something will happen" can be felt. Pure trust without an object.

Three weeks later, this person called my friend. He had gone half way across the country and tells her he is now ready to come home. The moment I heard about the call, the immediate heart-sensing of the world-action of the contemplation was felt.

This kind of occurrence actually poses a difficulty for contemplative action, for there seems to be an inner, almost causal connection between placing the image-presence of this person in the heart and something that later occurs. It was not felt that way. Noticing the particular qualities of the experience becomes important. News of his appearance was felt, not as a result of the contemplation, but rather as the continual unfolding of a complex picture involving this person and his wife and life and the world. The heartful action now asks that this complex picture be held in contemplation. Rather than feeling at an end of the contemplative action, this moment begins a different ongoing relation with these two people that now includes these two people and the world. What occurred — the disappearance of the man, the concern of his wife — are no long something isolated from a more comprehensive world-unfolding. I do not understand it and do not need to.

When we perceive someone's subtle presence within the heart, a mirroring of that presence occurs as the soul of that individual or event exists both in the cosmic world and within the depths of the Earthly world — combined. The "Above" and the "Below" come into appearance in the middle, the region of the heart. What appears, appears *through* the mirroring of heart imagination, but is not *in* the mirror. When image-feelings occur through the heart, they are very different than imagining from the mind, for mental images are already distant from the immediacy of their origination. The *power* of the heart synthesizes an unbounded unity into the felt heart-presence.

~

The power of the heart makes contemplative action possible by condensing into intense feeling, within the center of the heart, whatever attentiveness brings to focus.

The power of heart-focus consists of holding some specific image while feeling the whole contextual realm of spirit and soul presences composing who or what is held in heart. In heart, we are able to be completely with something or someone, not to the exclusion of everything else — as is required, for example, in concentration of the mind — but focus by total inclusion. Whatever heart focuses does so by including the individualized sense of the whole within the focus. Unless we at least have a feeling for the ways the heart follows laws that are different from those of mere physicalness, we are bound to reduce a most remarkable occurrence to something mundane.

~

The heart not only holds something or someone within, in focus, but does so by a genuine second creating of that presence. Heart births what is being imagined. Heart is inherently a creating capacity. It does not create "out of nothing," nor does it a make a mere resemblance, but for there to be anything or anyone within the heart's creative mirroring, the act of mirroring occurs. This is easy to verify. If you hold someone within your heart, you will notice that this holding is accompanied by the act of attention doing the holding. The act of attention is the creative act of the heart's imaginal mirroring.

~

~

The heart "images." "Image" does not mean that what or who we hold within the heart exists there as a picture, as something "visual-like." The word "image" comes from *imago*, and is very connected with the word "magic," as in "i-mage." When we say the heart "images," we mean that there is the "magical-like" presence within the heart of whatever is imagined. What we imagine is actually present, not as a representation of something somewhere else, but the reality exists within us — on its own terms, and according to its own laws, the laws of the heart. This power of the heart is one of the reasons imagination is excluded from the present world except in its fantasy form. It is too powerful, and the full mystery of imagination cannot be controlled by rationality, nor the techniques of fantasy.

~

~

The heart inherently "projects." Heart does not merely hold; its holding also constitutes the power of receptivity that enters the world as the action of the heart. Whatever heart imagines, under a certain condition — the condition of ardor — it endows what is being imagined with existence in the world. The action of the heart is not private.

~

When we enter into the Silence and place attention within the heart, letting attentiveness abide within heart, we notice, after a while, that while we began with the sense of placing our attention "inside," when we are "within" the heart, the heart is actually experienced as being "around us." Rather than heart being within us, we are within the heart. We do not have to do anything to have this happen except notice that it happens; it is not of our doing, but is of the nature of heart experience.

～

Becoming heart-capable involves intensifying the conscious presence of ardor of heart, the inherent love-action of the heart. Any time we enter the heart contemplatively, this quality is felt. The feeling is experienced, and along with it a sense of joy guides one toward more constant heart-presence. If ardor of heart does not intensify, heart-presence stops at the stage of sentimentality, an indication that ego consciousness has stepped in too early.

～

Orienting Toward Ardor of the Heart

The heart projects whatever is reflected within it. This is the ardor of the heart. What is heart-imagined produces changes in the world; it becomes "external" to us. Right here is where power immediately wants to seize and convert this reality to something utilitarian. If that happens, a different kind of projection occurs, psychic projection, which is illusion. The word "projection," in relation to the heart, is used here in the alchemical sense of the word. When alchemists came to a certain point of the alchemical operations, it then became possible to "project" the stone into the world. That is, alchemical transformation entered the world and became world transformation.

The difference between sentimentality and utilitarian use-orientation, and the heart's ardor, lies in purification. Sentimental heart-presence makes us, and perhaps others, feel better; but it does not do anything in the world except perhaps indirectly — if we feel better, our actions are probably more effective. Use-oriented heart-presence brings willfulness to the heart, which the heart will not receive, and the capacities of heartfulness recede. Ardor of heart does not mix with these other qualities, and as long as these other qualities are felt, ardor cannot be felt. The moment, then, we feel either of these qualities approaching

— desire or willfulness — we can find the way through distractions by returning, again and again, to heart-attentiveness.

The most favorable place to practice sensing ardor is in relation with the Natural World, for an infinite attraction exists between heart awareness and Nature.

Enter the Heart Alignment, and then into the Silence and Heart-Awareness. Then open your eyes, and be present within your surroundings. With attention, focus on something, like a cloud, or a tree, or a stone, while at the same time allowing your peripheral vision to be wide, into the periphery. This is a simultaneous "focus-diffuse" sensing. After a few minutes, close your eyes and notice the manner in which what you are with in the Natural World now lives within the place of the heart. There may be light, or an image, or movement, most certainly strong feeling.

While present with that inner imagining of a specific aspect of the Natural World, have attention focused in the heart — and in an act of active-receptivity, allow the feeling within the heart to flow into the inner attentiveness. With a very, very gentle act of the will, increase the intensity of that heart-feeling flowing into the inner attentiveness, through rhythmically breathing this heart-feeling into the attentiveness. This heart-feeling is not an emotion; it is a strongly felt "urgency" of love within the heart, as if there is an unending force within the heart that is autonomous from you, though also the most intimate aspect of you. Attentiveness does not occur outside the heart either; it is not as if the forces of attention are looking on to what goes on within the heart. Heart-attentiveness seems to inhere within the heart, but can be felt as a force that, while in inner connection with the heart's imagining, can also affect it.

Notice what begins to occur. When the inner attentiveness is approached from love within the heart, and love approaches attentiveness, the inner presence, the felt image of what or who we're with, responds. Warmth can be felt within the heart, and the warmth increases, maybe even warming the body. This warmth permates and embraces the image being held within the heart. An attraction forms between the warmed image and the felt sense of light within the heart, and in that moment, we feel that the image-presence is also a world presence. Invisible, but palpably present. It is as if the released image now finds its relation with the wholeness of the world, and this occurrence is the world action of the heart.

Do this practice in some sort of rhythm — once a day at the same time, for example. Do it for a month, maybe two, until there comes a point when it seems to live within you, has become a part of your very being.

~

The action of the true will-of-the-heart in the world, is the action of virtue. The ardor of the heart becomes the hands and feet of world action. Ardor of heart is not a function, nor is it a faculty, but a light. It is not intellect or will, but the background of our being, an immensity that cannot be possessed. From within the heart, a light shines through us upon things.

~

HEART AND EARTH

~

Capacities to perceptually experience Earth as Earth-soul through heart-centered awareness are now arising. These capacities unfold as a result of contemplative engagement with the heart. Earth has entered a new octave, and only now can these capacities be developed.

~

~

The travails of Earth and her creatures are now acute, and we fear that Earth may not survive. Nor will we. The only way through such a hugely dire situation requires that heart-attention join awareness with Earth. We are, at any rate, Earth's awareness, though we are not yet conscious of being so, for our acts of domination blind us. We act as if we are Earth-independent, that She is our servant, that we conquer Nature.

~

～

That illusion of our being other than Earth, rather than Earth-beings, has entered the end-time. A mythic picture of this moment occurs in the Book of Revelation:

Next appeared a great portent in heaven, a woman robed with the sun, beneath her feet the moon, and on Her head a crown of Twelve Stars. She is pregnant, and in the anguish of her labor she cried out to be delivered.

— Revelation, 12:1-2

The woman here is the soul of Earth, who has been called Sophia, Wisdom, who, in giving birth to her own spirit assumes, for the first time, the fullness of individual being. Earth-soul does not abandon her own soul. She does not let Earth become mere "matter," and ultimately, Earth is not subject to the laws of physical matter as we have concocted those laws through materialistic physics and heartless greed. Under these circumstance, the more subtle aspects of the unity of Earth with the heart of humans goes unnoticed.

～

～

This is the age of the opening of the heart in a more collective way, for only through the forces of the heart can humanity become aware of the travails Earth undergoes, to actually feel Earth as a living Being, and consciously join our being with hers. Otherwise, we continue falling into a literalized spell of the events of the Book of Revelation as the unveiling of the end.

～

～

The Book of Revelation speaks mythically, in the true sense of myth as something that never happened but is always happening. The Book of Revelation is a myth of the future — the future as always happening, always coming-into-being. This destined future does not happen without us, but it is not something that we can do; we can only be receptive to this monumental moment of time, or, in rejecting it, seal our future as dire. Earth-soul evolving into Earth-Human heart-presence portends a great unity, with awareness, one that can always be felt occurring, but not yet grasped in its significance.

～

—

Earth's becoming Human-Earth-Soul can only be felt and perceived through the heart, through the kind of consciousness that reveals what is actual and present, without the literalizing characteristic of "usual" consciousness. This mode of consciousness is *imaginal*. No notion of "imaginary," or fantasy, is intended. Imaginal consciousness characterizes the act of being simultaneously within the Silence, within heart awareness, with others, receptive, and Earth-present.

—

～

Don't you already feel Earth's Nature as taking Her own course? Doesn't this seem to be the beginning of the end? "The end of Earth" — so say the climate prophets, but they really, unknowingly, mean the beginning of the end of acting as if heart were not the united center of our being and Earth-being, and the ending of how we have lived the illusion of conquering Nature.

～

～

The rose is without an explanation;

She Blooms, because She Blooms.

— Angelus Silesius (1624-1677)

Angelus Silesius speaks as if inspired by Sophia, for he writes a perfect description of Her here, as if She is the Rose of the World. She reveals Herself without a "why," coursing within everything of Nature, within Earth, within human body and soul, down to the core.

～

～

The multiple expressivenesses of Sophia as Earth becoming self-aware, and all who surround and embrace Her as Queen of Creation, all are what they are, without a why. Learning to live without a why, unfolding within the Whole, as a rose does — this will characterize the age of Sophia. We see it now, clearly, when we perceive directly the beings of Nature. They all come-to-be, each moment, the symphony of Earth's heart awareness.

～

Every mineral, crystal, and precious stone exists as a creative flowering of hundreds of creating spiritual and elemental beings — of heaviness, reflection, color, shape, inclusions, brittleness or malleability. Every plant exists, wholly, within Wholeness, with hundreds of thousands of both cosmic and Earth-spiritual creating presences of form, color, root, stem flower, seed, leaf, fruit, a communion of Earth Wholeness. Every animal exists as the expressed Wholeness of up to a million or more creating presences of form — hair, eyes, teeth, hoofs, gestures, and the rhythmic presences of all the internal organs and physiology as well. The human being: a Wholeness of the Wholeness of millions of creating presences.

~

All that we sense and perceive and inwardly feel of Earth within the region of the heart are Earth as soul presence and simultaneously every individual Earth being, whether mineral, plant, animal, or human — each in its own Feeling dimension.

~

Stones feel, plants feel, animals feel, and humans feel. We have to use this common word "feel" to rightly express that all matter feels, the soul-essence of all matter feels. The interior touching together of soul with matter, the action of that union, is Feeling. There are not, within this Earth-Centered, Sophia-Centered way of Wisdom, "things," that then feel, but the soul nature of their Being is the activity of Feeling, the "oneing" of cosmos-earth-human soul.

For us, who are so overly-cognized and cognize about everything, usually a form of cognizing that seals every presence within itself — for us, hearing that stones, plants, animals, and humans exist as soul-feeling-presences and can be known on their own terms, in their totality, through heart-feeling, begins to stretch and even threaten the position of rationality as "all-knower."

—

We know, don't we, that stones do not feel? And while much research exists revealing that plants do feel, it is "off the edge" of acceptable knowing. We can perhaps admit that animals have a certain level of feeling-instinct. And, yes, humans have feelings. The imaginations of this book, however, do not speak of "having" feelings, but rather of Feeling as constituting the mode of creating presence of Earth-soul as if she knows herself as in union with refined human-awareness in making the symphony of Earth as vibratory, before the existence of objects which vibrate.

—

～

The vibrations are the arising of things with soul, not the other way around. If indeed the tradition is correct in naming Sophia the Soul of the World, Her presence as Earth is vibratory and all-inclusive. "Vibratory," however, is but the outward characteristic of the soul quality of Feeling.

～

～

Feeling knows by union. Union precedes separation. Earth-soul does not take multiple known things and put them together into one, resulting in, as the cliché often used today says, "Everything is related with everything else." Such a sense of union tries to comprehend unity from the outside. Earth-soul lives within and as sensorially felt Wholeness, and thus remains invisible to those who do not notice the feeling dimension, and a plethora of Beauty for those who can.

～

CLEANING THE MEMORY MIRROR
OF SENSING EARTH

Sense-feeling of Earth-soul requires loosening the ways that immediate perceiving is always guided by what we already know. We know, for example, "what trees are." This knowing completely pervades our perceiving.

On a walk, find a place that attracts you. Walk rather aimlessly and without a goal in mind; you will notice some particular aspect of the world that the body feels in connection with — a stone, a plant, a flower, a tree, grass, a plant.

In that place, attend to all that you can notice — everything that you take in through sensory presence.

See-feel-heart-smell — notice colors, weight, alignment, movement, stillness, light — and try to take it in all at once, rather than piecemeal.

Notice both the exterior objects and what you are sensing, and any feelings you may experience, any images or fantasies, intuition, memories, whatever occurs.

Begin to inwardly slowly strip away, one at a time, the characteristics of what you sensed and felt — strip away the "what" of what you sensed. For example, if you felt the particularity of a certain tree, now strip away the tree as it exists within your experience; strip away the colors seen, the sounds heard, the movements seen and felt, the memories, the images, the fantasies, down to the felt presence of Earth — down to that ever-present "place" where you always are. Strip away everything you can possibly imagine that connects you with matter. Let all this collapse into nothing.

Stay as long as possible with the nothing. Feel the Silence.

Now, place attention within the heart and feel the Silence — allow all that was stripped away to now be heart-present within the Silence.

This practice imitates the action of Earth. It is like planting a seed. When we put a seed in the ground, it is as if all we knew of that plant disappears into the darkness, as if all we know is suddenly stripped away. Here, in the darkness, a mysterious process occurs. The seed completely disintegrates. At the exact moment of its complete disintegration, Life begins. A very similar process occurs whenever we place something within the heart — all we knew and thought we knew, all we see, remember, think about, all that brings emotion, fantasy — all this disappears at the moment of the re-birthing of Earth, from within the human heart.

—

This prayer/practice, done repeatedly, with care, loosens the "known Earth" and opens bodily sensing of Earth-Human-Soul presence. Knowing, pre-conceptions, images, fantasies, memories, begin to yield to presence, to and within Earth Feeling. This kind of experience unfolds slowly. We may, at first, only notice a brief moment of the presence of Earth Feeling as different than "having feelings." Because Feeling is its own way of "knowing," it cannot be captured by cognition, and thus easily slips away, like a dream. Gradually we become more able to live within this kind of "Earth-conversing."

—

~

We can begin to live with Earth as the "great unknown." Each moment can be filled with revelation as we continue with practices of softly keeping at bay what we already know. Then, more subtle, inherently receptive qualities come to the fore — humility, trust, affirmation, truthfulnesss. Earth herself reveals herself as these kinds of qualities — the eternal "Yes" of the Earth-soul. As we allow Earth presence to fill us rather than keeping Feeling at bay through "pre-knowing" everything, we bodily enter into an inherent morality. We cannot harm Earth without it being harm to every creature and harm to the Human. This morality has nothing to do with "good" versus "bad"; it consists of the immediate felt quality of everything, without exception, beginning with all Earth-presences as one, while the particularity of each aspect remains.

~

~

Our first and enduring conversation is with Earth, for we are always with Her and She is always with us. This primordial conversation reveals that we live, before "knowing," within a very different cosmology than the cosmologies we have concocted, particularly the cosmology of the "Big Bang." Such a cosmology has no room for an Earth-Soul, and even less than "no room" for Earth-Human-Soul.

If everything begins with a gigantic explosion, this explosion becomes the template for everything of Earth. The theory locating explosion as the beginning, continues, now being fulfilled as violence, combustion engines, rockets, war, Earth-destruction, conflagration, anger, conflict, natural catastrophes, nuclear melt-down, politics, terrorism, guns, guns, and more guns, cursing, and hatred.

We do not need to know physics to be caught in this unstoppable destructiveness, for the archetype of this kind of physics encompasses us all, and we live within the capture of this cosmology, keeping itself as pure destruction-in-the-making, hidden under the guise that technology will get us out of the mess we have created.

~

Rudolf Steiner once said, "The physicist's atom does not exist." This most interesting statement does not say, "Atoms do not exist." He is likely saying that the atom conceived as particles that are at the same time energy — electrons, protons, neutrons, and all the rest of the purely materialistic structures and action — that atom does not exist. As long as we live within that cosmology, Sophia, Earth-soul, does not exist — except as myths, memories, philosophical longings, and the actual visions of a few who have undergone religious experiences, now revered only as religious idolatry, rather than the charged presence of Earth Herself.

—

The word "physics" originates from the Greek *physis*, which means "to be born," so physics is the language of Earth being born . . . each moment, of Earth's coming- to-be — but certainly not as the combination of the physicist's atom.

—

~

The physicist's atom is an artifact of the way of investigation. Scientific proof of the structure of the atom began by bombarding the atom with light; as they did so, the atom disappeared in the light. So they excited the atom with strong magnetic and electric fields which speeded atoms up, causing an alteration of the atom itself. Atom means "indivisible." Electrons, protons, neutrons, positrons, and so on are products of the *altered* atom. Thus the laws of the atom are unwittingly altered. We then have "theoretical physics" seemingly verified, which as theories always do, prove themselves without recognizing that the proofs partake of the same assumptions as the theories.

The word "physics" is indeed a beautiful word — the being-born of Earth. Earth, Sophia, coming-to-be human, with individualized awareness. We are Earth's awareness, who, with our intrinsic freedom, easily separate from the paradox of being integrally, spiritually united with Earth — and independent beings at the same time.

~

—

No separation between Human and Earth is possible. No matter how far we seem to be from Earth, we are always in intimate conversation with Her, through our feet, even when subjecting Her to terrible dissections based on physics or chemistry or biology or medicine or atomic physics or digitalization. She bears, silently, whatever we do in our ignorance, being-born as also bearing, carrying, just as the Sophia of the Apocalypse bears her own birth as spirit-Earth, and just as she bears all that happens to the Earth we think we know.

—

～

The essence of Sophianic Earth cosmology centers within the atom's intrinsic existence as Rhythm, rather than the nuclear physicists' atom. The atom as the most basic forming of all matter, exists as Rhythm. Atoms vibrate as whole harmonic rhythms rather than miniature universes complexly circling forms of energy. And atoms are, in their own way, awareness-filled. Only the materialist has to ponder how to get to consciousness from pure materiality. A cosmology that resonates with everything spoken of in this writing locates awareness as inherent, from the beginning.

～

～

Rhythmic cosmology imagines creation as originating from cosmic Light condensing into vibration pouring through the cosmos, and a returning Luminous Light emerging from Earth, of a lower frequency/vibration. The constant coming together of these primordial currents, in their eternal entwining, differing in frequency of vibration, produces the never-ending current of Rhythmic creating as it comes into Being, or Wholeness. Only one completely unknown physicist, Pier Luigi Ighina, knew of these rhythms and was able to create incredible receptive devices utilizing Rhythm, including devices for preventing earthquakes, for gathering rainstorms, for agriculture, and for healing. The evidence he presented showing the practicality of this physics was summarily rejected, as it did not fit in with what physicists "know."

～

———

With "Big Bang" it's all about speed, while with Rhythmic Cosmology it is all about beauty and presence. With "Big Bang," a physics of speedy atoms and particles, and being sucked into black holes, tells the dramatic story. With Rhythmic Cosmology, the essential nature of the atom is one of stillness and relation. Rhythmic Cosmology includes us who live within the rhythms of attentiveness, and who are also gently being tended, the two-as-one, within vibration.

———

—

Heartfulness has a difficult time unless we develop full confidence in the truth of immediacy, and unless we, each moment, feel our feet in intimate union with Earth.

Deep Silence certainly has nothing to do with speed. If we think of the Silence as a void, emptiness, being stopped, slowing down, entering the "non-practical," such views are how it feels if we try to enter the Silence from the cosmology of speed. Everything goes away. A kind of modern physicists' mystical state. But from within Rhythmic Cosmology, the Silence is alive, palpably felt, extremely active in its own ways, and signifies Wholeness, always in readiness to reconfigure into moments of rhythmic presences. This kind of cosmology goes together with deep heart-listening; if what we speak has no inherent Silence, we cannot listen. We can only take in what we literally heard, cognize it, and utilize it, such as we do with information, for information has no Silence, but only speed.

—

~

All is alive and vital, expressed with Rhythmic intensities, specific to each form and each individual expression of Life. If there is no Rhythm, life cannot exist. But, we cannot confine "life" to biological life. Rhythm not only characterizes the existence of living beings, but also of all that appears in the created universe.

~

⁓

From within heart-presence, Rhythm is experienced as subtle pulsations of expansion and contraction. These pulsations are not merely the heart's own rhythms, but are felt pulsations of everything.

Because we are not accustomed to being heart-present — that is, being Earth-soul present — when we feel the heart at all, we feel an outer sense of external, alternating beats of the heart. When we enter into the Silence and Heart-Awareness, we begin to be present to the utter particularities of the world. A rose, for example, is not just a rose; each rose presents a unique rhythm, perceptually present. A tree, for example, a pine tree — which looks as if static because we see it through cognitive perceiving — can be experienced Rhythmically, through the Silence of heart in immediate, sensory-soul attentiveness. When we do feel, centered in heart, fully bodily present, the tree becomes "this" living being, with all its unique and specific qualities, with unending depth, the specific rhythms experienced as Beauty.

⁓

＊

Being Earth-soul present easily degenerates into noticing only the beauty of Earth-soul, and would leave her travails aside, unnoticed, hoping that, somehow, all the difficulties we see Earth going through will be alleviated by external means — science, technology, ecology, activism, research. All these resources, however, have already been garnered in the opposite direction. New forms of action will be required, actions from within Earth-soul cosmology, heart-action. Nothing can change while captured within a cosmology that begins everything with explosiveness. At the very most, without change of consciousness, the destructive process can be slightly slowed down with care and technology.

＊

BEARING THE TRAVAILS OF EARTH

Begin with inward presence with some devastating event — a large forest fire, a tsunami, oil spill, water contamination, poaching tigers or elephants . . . whatever first comes to you.

Be inwardly present with such a moment through inner images. Allow yourself to enter into the images . . . become the images, feel the grieving . . . it is yours and also it is Earth's. You can best feel such images from within heart-presence and the Silence, and at the same time, with attention placed in the region of the feet. You will feel currents emerging from the Earth, and shortly qualities of grieving will be felt. Then, allow the felt grief to be filled with a specific image of what Earth bears.

Allow the felt image, with the grieving, to come to the inner surface of the heart.

Notice that a stilling of the disturbing images occurs. Disturbance is not blocked out, denied, or removed. The stilling holds all of the qualities of the images, but now in the Stillness of the heart instead of the trembling of emotion. Stay within this stillness of images for a while.

Then, allow your attention to be with the stillness of the images, and with your attentiveness, the soft will of attentiveness, move the image-complex to the center of the heart. Feel the images right at the center of the heart. It takes little effort for this movement to take place. If you find that it takes effort, you are likely now, in attentiveness, within the images, but have distanced yourself from them and are as if "looking at them." Go back to the previous step, and proceed again.

At the center of the heart lies a quality of "golden light." It may not be actually "light," but it has the feeling quality of golden light — warm, soft, bright, filled with levity. Again, the devastating images are not erased. They are now bathed in the qualities of the center of the heart, and now, even within this "darkness," a creative force can be noticed. Stay here for a while.

Then, allow your attention to be at the back of the heart. The back of the heart feels like the opening to an unending vortex with the felt quality of the action of love. It is not sentimental or emotional love, but rather the force of love. Allow the images, with soft attentiveness, to move into the depth at the back of the heart. Stay there for a while.

Then, begin to allow the images to move, first, from the back of the heart. The images feel decidedly different. Filled with creative force. Then, allow the images *to move into the golden light at the center of the heart. The images garner levity there, and are felt again as belonging here, with the Earth, whereas at the back of the heart, all goes into depth-force.*

Then, allow the images to move to the surface of the heart. The devastation of the images has not gone away, it is still present — now you bear what is happening, but it does not feel that you are bearing the devastation alone. Sometimes when there is great ardor of heart with this practice, at this place of the inner surface of the heart, visions of your particular engagement with the healing of Earth appear and can be felt.

~

No ending of heartfulness concludes this writing. This last imaginal prayer portrays what we have come to.

~

The Prayer/Practices

1. Heart Alignment

"Hail to the brow!" With eyes closed, place attention there, right at the center, and inwardly feel the simultaneity of expanse into an infinite sphere with unending depth, both at once, open and free, fluid. Remain here for several minutes. Remain at each phase for a few moments as it unfolds.

"Hail to the throat!" Allow attentiveness its natural flow from the brow as attention moves to the region of the throat. Notice the stillness of the brow as it moves to the throat, now felt as the most subtle inner sensation of inner movement here — as if holy speaking, silent, radiates from the region of the throat, while remaining clear and centered.

"Hail to the heart!" Allow attention to move to this center, continuing the flow from brow to throat, arriving at the place where heart-as-experienced originates simultaneous inner presence with radiance. Warmth, intimacy, unity, and circulation of sacredness are felt here. Allow attention here to flow "back" to the region of the throat and to the region of the brow, and "down again," to heart.

"Hail to the Solar Plexus!" Allow attention to move to the top of the stomach, toward the back. Notice attention here, flowing from the heart, into the very

center of will. The explosive, outward "I will" — felt now as the power of pure receptivity.

Allow attention to slowly and rhythmically flow, upward through each center, and downward. These holy body centers differ from "chakras"; they are centers of aligning attention, retrieving us from scatteredness on the one hand and excessive single-centeredness on the other. Notice how we feel centered, "here," full, present, within a pervading, always-present silence as the prayer/practice concludes.

2. The Silence

With eyes closed, place attention at any specific region at the periphery of the body. For example, place attention at the edge of your right arm. Notice what that feels like: it is as if you are being lightly touched by the Silence that always encompasses and embraces our bodily existence, transforming biology into spirit-soul-body presence.

Shift attention to another peripheral place of the body, such as the edge your left leg. Notice again the very palpable presence of the Silence, as if being lightly touched by an invisible, caressing presence.

Then, as you shift attention to various peripheral places of the body, notice how the Silence announces itself wherever attention occurs. You feel as if being lightly touched, subtly embraced, touched by invisibility — body relaxes, tightness eases, expansion occurs, body-awareness increases in intensity, and the existence of a new sensation occurs, the sensation of healing, of coming into wholeness.

When noticing the Silence at the periphery of the body, feel what that is like for a while, then, at one of the bodily peripheral places, with your attention, enter into that exact region where you noticed what the Silence is like. In this act of "entering," of allowing your attention to flow into the bodily-felt silence, you identify completely with the Silence, you become the Silence. You pour your being into the Silence. What was experienced a moment ago as a subtle sensation now becomes intimately felt from within. The particular peripheral body-location of the Silence yields to an all-pervasive subtle sensing that is the presence of the Silence.

3. Gesturing "Heart"

As the ease and comfortableness of the Silence adjust, we enter the heart through another form of resonance. We do not just go from the Silence into heart awareness.

Within the Silence, with your lips, silently gesture, speak, the word "heart." An immediate and fairly strong bodily resonating of the word occurs and it is as if the whole of the Silence reconfigures itself as an intense, felt silence at the place of the heart.

At this place of strong bodily resonance we gently place attention within the center of the heart. Stay within the heart for as long as it remains comfortable. If anxiousness arises, try to remain within the heart, not by fighting against the anxiety, but by returning each moment to heart awareness. Complete this contemplation whenever you like. It will feel like we never want to leave.

4. Heart-Awareness

Take a flower, but one that is not particularly beautiful or outstanding in any way, an ordinary flower, and carefully observe it. (After working with a flower for several weeks, you can change to something else — a stone, for example.) Hold the flower in your hand and look at it with tending care, turning it over, seeing it from all sides. After doing this observation for a few minutes, make an inner image of the flower.

At first it is likely that this will be a mental image of the flower. You can tell it if is a mental image if you "see" the flower with your interior eye as if you are looking at the flower; that is, you mentally see only one side of the flower.

Allow the image to move down into the interior of your heart; that is, now "see" the flower with the heart's eye. You will have the feeling of seeing all sides of the flower at once, something like a hologram. It is not a literal "seeing," but more like feeling — a felt, but quite precise sense of the flower, occurring within the heart as feeling that is like a "seeing."

Simply hold the flower in heart awareness for a few minutes . . . Then, consciously erase the image of the flower and remain in the empty void as long as you can. Then open your eyes.

This contemplation enacts a surrendering to the nature and laws of the imaginal heart, the heart of felt substance and the substance of felt heart, breaking through our literalized notions of the heart as a substance without metaphor and a metaphor without substance.

5. Sensory Heart-Awareness

Begin by noticing heartfulness through aligning, opening into the Silence, and gesturing the word "heart." Then, allow the usual awareness of sound to be felt as sound-awareness by noticing something, such as a bird singing or the clank of something metal, move from its seeming location at the place of the ears, to also moving outward from the heart-awakened body, toward the source of what you hear. You hear a bird singing; you allow the rhythmic sound to also be felt as if originating from the heart-awakened body toward the bird, and back. This prayer/practice, as with each of the prayer/practices, simply notices the actual happening — in this case of sound. We do not try to make something happen with the prayer/practices, but rather take up now an ongoing unfolding of tuning our new embodiment.

6. Pure Body-Awareness

As with all prayer/practices, begin by sitting in a quiet place where you will not be disturbed, and close your eyes.

Begin this practice by doing the Heart Alignment and shifting your awareness to the place of the heart. Then, go into the Silence. Let your attention notice the area surrounding your body. Feel the presence of the currents of the Silence, which are like being gently touched, felt at the body periphery.

When you feel these currents, switch your attention to the interior of your body, to the interior space of the body, to the currents of the Silence there. This feels as if the interior is an empty, but substantial space. The Silence within the interior of the body is qualitatively different than the Silence surrounding and penetrating the body. It is deeper, much deeper, endlessly deep, whereas the Silence surrounding the body has the quality of infinite expanse.

When you have that sense of the interior of the Silence of the body, switch your attention again to the outside surrounding your body. With your attention, switch back and forth a number of times. At first, this "switching" is difficult. If it does not feel difficult, then it is likely that you are doing the "switching" only mentally.

When you switch from interior to exterior and back, it has to be done bodily; that is, when you "intend" the switch, you also feel it resonating bodily. You can feel that this is an effort of the receptive will, rather than simply "thinking about it."

When the switching has occurred several times, dissolve the feeling of the presence of a thin "membrane" separating interior and exterior currents of the Silence, and you are within Pure Body-Awareness. The boundary of the skin as encasing body seems removed, and yet no sense of being "out of body" results. We feel completely bodied, and yet do not experience the bounded form of our body.

7. "Sealing" Heart-Awareness

Do the Heart Alignment prayer/practice. Then "seal" it by gesturing the words "Brother Heart Alignment."

These words resonate deeply and strongly within the subtle body, and the Heart Alignment resonates through the body, moving down the centers as when inwardly speaking each step. Then, the next time you are going to do the Heart Alignment, you just gesture the words "Brother Heart Alignment," noticing how the whole alignment happens without having to go through the entire process. It is the presences that were doing the aligning all along, but we were not yet receptive enough to notice, and instead thought that we were "doing something," rather than invoking the help of spiritual presences.

Then, from time to time, to check up and strengthen the whole, do the entire Heart Alignment as described earlier, followed by gesturing the words, "Brother Heart Alignment." Otherwise, after a while, the mind does its tricky thing and the sealing gesture reverts to being only outer words lacking interior resonance.

While all of the prayer/practices presented thus far are crucial, once a level of comfort with them occurs, so that we are no longer "self-instructing" ourselves in order to feel what the practices are doing, then these key prayer/practices can be sealed, as indicated with the Heart Alignment. The sealing can be developed in the following way:

Do each of the prayer/practices, followed with gesturing these words:

Heart Alignment — "Brother Heart Alignment"

The Silence at the periphery of the body — "Sister Silence"

The Silence within the interior of the body — "Brother Silence"

Pure Body-Awareness — "Brother-Sister Pure Body-Awareness"

Heart-Awareness — "Sister Heart-Awareness"

8. Heart-Presence With Another Person

To begin a prayer/ practice that initiates heart-relating as an ongoing way of being present with others, ask someone you know to simply sit with you for a little while:

With your eyes closed, enter the Sealing prayer/practice as developed earlier. (Alternately, do the four key prayer/practices in full.) Then, open your eyes and simply be within your heart with the other person. Without speaking, remain within the felt sense of heartfulness with the other person, until you feel it fade.

9. Mutual Heart-Presence

Start with the Heart Alignment, the Silence, Heart-Awareness — or enter into the Sealing prayer/practice. As you now face the person from within heartfulness, place your visual attention at a specific place, such as a button on the shirt of the other person, something innocuous; we are not engaged in mutual "gazing," we do not seem, nor do we "try" to make something happen. As sensory focus centers on a particular place, at the same time, allow your vision to peripherally extend beyond the bodily form of the other person. Let your vision be simultaneously focused at the one place, while diffusely extending even beyond the person. At first, this kind of sensation may seem odd, and even be a kind of strain. During this prayer/ practice, for the time being, both individuals remain silent.

Within a few minutes, in becoming accustomed to this "focus-diffuse" sensing, an utterly innocent "merging" with the other person occurs, as if the space between you can be felt. When you feel this moment of the subtlety of unity, close your eyes and allow the feeling presence of the other person to continue. (Before beginning this prayer/practice, you might want to tell the other person of this process and invite the other person to close her/his eyes when you close yours, and just be present.)

It is as if you and the other person are being held within an embrace of intimacy, an intimacy unlike any felt before. No entanglement whatsoever occurs. Both you and the other person remain completely free, and in fact, what happens in meeting in this way concerns the initial waking-up within our bodily-emotional freedom. Instead of the scary and entirely premature and inappropriate possibility of emotional entanglement that immediately makes one want to pull away, we experience the full and true holiness that is this person. We do so through the center of the true holiness of our own Being. We awaken to and within our and the other's personhood. We experience, directly, sensorily, the other-as-person, through the heart as medium of our personhood.

10. Speaking With Another Person
Within Heart-Presence

Ask your friend if she or he will enter the place of the heart with you again. Then indicate that this time what you are both going to try and do is to speak aloud with each other while being consciously focused within the heart. This means that while one person is speaking, the other person remains fully within heart-presence while listening; the same thing occurs when there is the switching of who is talking and who is listening. The first time doing this, it is helpful to choose something to speak about. Suggest, for example, that you speak together about what brings you joy.

11. Heart-Listening Within Nature

Take a walk. Begin to listen while being within the Silence and heart-presence. Seeing, walking, touching, hearing, smelling, being within the plethora of sensing and being within the heart — all are modes of listening with Nature. Attempt to listen to the deep Silence of the physical world — not the given physical world as you typically notice it. Notice how the Silence is very different as you stand and simply notice, from within heart-presence, a tree, and then a boulder, or a plant, moving water, a breeze, or anything else of Nature. Each presence emerges from the Silence as a particular expressing of the Silence. Even each particular thing — one tree, and next to it another tree of the same kind, speak the Silence very individually.

12. Heart-Listening With Earth

Make a descent into the soul-body by shifting attention that is habitually located in the region of the head to the region of the heart. Notice that you sense the Silence, and through the Silence, sense the Earthly soul/spirit particularity of where you stand or sit. Then, while attention can be felt in the heart, simultaneously place attention in the region of the feet. When you speak with someone — in an instant, but with felt body-ness — re-enact this descent.

13. Heart-Listening With Heart-Earth-Another Person

Sit with a friend within the Silence of the heart. Notice the tonality that you, together, create, through noticing your body-presence while sensing Earth-presence. Speak with each other, trying to speak the qualities of being together in this way without losing the felt sense of the tonality. Avoid interpreting what you think body experiences. Experience the speaking of the other in its gestural manifestation. Do not be concerned about understanding each other, for that will produce a shifting into cognition.

14.   Listening for the Emerging Word

Engage with a prayer/practice of speaking together with someone while maintaining the Silence, not only while listening to the other person, but within your own speaking.

Notice the tendency of speaking to "get ahead of itself." When we begin to feel we are waiting to say something we want to say, let attention return more deeply into the Silence. Listen inwardly for the emerging creation of what wants to speak, rather than what we want to speak.

Feel the bodily field and feel how what the other person says lives within us, bodily, rather than understood mentally. Allow words to come with their own rhythm and timing, which will occur, quite naturally, much slower than a mental pace.

15. Finding the Heart-Space of Reverent Waiting

Go into the Silence and place attention in the center of the heart. Then, make an image, seeing yourself inwardly, lying on your back, floating on a clear, calm lake.

Be within this image — go into it. There will come a moment when you actually feel that you are floating on a clear, calm lake. The body will be floating there. As long as you are present within this sensation of floating on the lake, your mind will be clear and not occupied with thinking. You have given consciousness something "to do" that is not thinking. You will be able to notice, "out of the corner of your consciousness" as you are floating on the clear, calm lake, the complete relaxation of the body — and also what the "empty mind, full-heart" feels like. Once we bodily experience this "waiting space," it becomes ever easier to find when with others.

16.   Heart-Listening Within Conflict

When conflict with someone begins:

l. Take a breath: Inhale and identify within you what is upsetting you.

2. Let go of it as you exhale.

3. Second breath: Inhale and feel the Silence at the center of your being.

4. Exhale.

5. Third breath: Inhale and ask yourself inwardly "What's next?" Listen. Exhale and notice what emerges.

17. Transforming Emotional Reaction
Into Heartful Emotion

Begin with writing a narrative of an emotional memory — what occurred, what the emotion is like, what was the outcome.

As you read the story, notice how the egotizing of emotion relies a great deal on the "skimming" of a memory — that is, omitting important but consciously available details of the memory. So, the second step, after writing the emotional memory-narrative, is to go back, enter the presence of the memory from the place of the Silence and the region of the heart, feeling the embrace of Earth, and notice where absent details begin to be available. Make notes of these details, which is the first "acknowledgement" of the holiness of the memory itself — the recognition that there is more to what occurred than the ego is wanting us to see.

In the "expanding" memory — that is, as the memory frees from the egotizing reactionary process — the sense of the "memory" as not really a memory at all, but an imaginal event that is happening, now emerges. As you feel the event happening now, however, you do not see yourself as the center of the emotion, as in the narration memory. When we are within an emotional event, we do not see ourselves, we are an aspect of a whole unfolding world — of another, or others, the surroundings, the light, the tonality of the moment, the sense of time. With the egotizing of the emotion, which occurs immediately, almost spontaneously, we become the center and the all. The emotion as flow gets covered and captured by ego to keep the memory stuck in repetitiveness, rather than emotion as the very force of spirit in life.

Repeat now, the breathing practice given earlier, with this purified imagination of the event. Notice being closer with the presence of the emotion, and to the spiritual emotion-body. From within the Silence and the heart, now re-live the emotion-event — saying what you said, saying what you were thinking, feeling the same feeling, gesturing with your body, letting the event "act" . . . again, however, doing so from within the Silence and being within the heart — giving the holy space necessary.

18. Meeting Ego

We begin with the Heart Alignment, and then allow attentiveness to appear within the interior of the heart. Then we enter the Silence and into Pure Body-Awareness and Heart-Awareness:

Imagine the presence of a being, who looks just like you, sitting with his/her back to your back, the backs touching each other. This being is of a subtle nature, so don't literalize the picture. It is both a felt sense of you, and you can picture the being as looking like you. The presence of this figure constitutes a variation of your individual spirit, the variation that can and does forget itself as a spiritual being, and instead tries to make its way through life on its own. We begin to get the sense of ego acting as if it were independent of the spiritual and soul realms.

Sit quietly, in the Silence. Then, let this presence glide like a breath through your body, touching every cell as it is moving from the back to the front. Let it move through you and then "float" in front of you. Look this presence in the eye (it will not be literally seen, much more felt) and admit its presence into the felt heart-field — the body-sensitivity that extends beyond the physical body. Be aware of the qualities, gestures, and features of this Being, no matter how difficult they might be. Let this being say what it wants to say to you. Hear it speak, though the hearing occurs within you, inaudibly, and may be more a feeling-sense than verbal. Let it tell you who it is and what it wants. Then, ask for the grace of change, that this presence does not dominate you unconsciously. Take time and let this unfold slowly. If you seem to be "making up" things, don't be concerned. Just notice.

After this is done, while you are sitting facing each other, feel the way in which both of you together form a rounded space with its midpoint between you.

Lead both figures — the ego and the immediate sense of your body — to this midpoint. Let them both lean slightly inward, into the vortex of the heart. Feel this movement. Be present to the qualities. The power of love that was previously frozen ego-awareness within begins feeling freed.

19. Meeting the "I" of Heartfulness

Make an inner image of your full being as an egg-shaped multi-colored mist of light extending outside, around, and through your physical body.

At the center of this mist is a tiny spark — your usual "I."

You — as "I Am" — has existence outside this egg. See it as a golden mist reaching down to your multi-colored being.

Sometimes it reaches the surface of your being; sometimes it withdraws into the universe.

See it as a flowing, continual movement, like gentle waves kissing the shore. Sometimes the sun glistens in this golden mist making it finer and lighter.

Sometimes the sunlit mist shines into your egg-shaped being as through a dark forest — engaging your small "I," that tiny spark at the center of your being.

The tiny spark starts to flicker within you, and grows, becoming one with the sunlit mist.

20. The "I Am" Mantras

To be inwardly, bodily-gesturally said from the place of the central point of the heart:

This I Am is a body of Light
I Am a body of Light

This I Am is a body of Silence
I Am a body of Silence

This I Am is a body of Love
I Am a body of Love

21. Heartful Action—Part I

Begin with entering into Heart Alignment, the Silence, and Heart-Awareness.

Once within Heart-Awareness, inwardly, within the heart, make an image of who or what situation or event you are working with. The difficult part from here on is to be able to relinquish, completely, any desire or need to want to change the person or the event or situation. Hold this inner image without a "why." If any desire to do something can be felt, release this desire, while nonetheless holding the image with the qualities of whatever is happening — that is, if a person is suffering, or the situation is one of illness or tragedy or need, hold that image, making it as you would see the situation in the world, but without any desire or need to change it.

To hold this image within the heart with heart-tending, this central creating place of the heart, place you right hand over the place of your heart. When heart-sensitiveness and attentiveness has developed through engaging the prayer/practices sufficiently, this small gesture unites the will with the heart.

This unity is strongly felt as an overwhelming sense of receiving the heart-held image touching the palm of your hand and radiating back into the heart.

Gesture the name of the person or the event being held in this way. Feel the image being held come into the radiance of the heart, as if the heart-space becomes inner light. When felt, any notion of taking this creative act and using it for our own purposes becomes impossible without breaking the felt unity of the heart-will. Gradually, through this simple contemplation, become used to the qualities of this small place of the heart, the very center of contemplative action.

Heartful Action—Part II

The second aspect involves now noticing the action aspect of the contemplation within the world. It may not show up immediately, but should do so within three days of the first part of the contemplative action. It will appear as a synchronicity. That is, something will occur within the world, usually the Natural World, that is unmistakably the presence of what you engaged in contemplation, though in a very different form. The content of what we notice is not the primary quality that informs us of this extraordinary moment of perceiving being at-one with the contemplation. It will be a strong, subtle response of recognition. We feel a distinct quality of being "befriended" by a presence — this may be a bird, a stone, something in the landscape, a person, some object, or something occurring — felt, though, as an action. In itself, it will not seem related to the contemplation, but you will know, without question, that it is. This is the action-dimension of the contemplative action.

22. Orienting Toward Ardor of the Heart

The most favorable place to practice sensing ardor is in relation with the Natural World, for an infinite attraction exists between heart awareness and Nature.

Enter the Heart Alignment, and then into the Silence and Heart-Awareness. Then open your eyes, and be present within your surroundings. With attention, focus on something, like a cloud, or a tree, or a stone, while at the same time allowing your peripheral vision to be wide, into the periphery. This is a simultaneous "focus-diffuse" sensing. After a few minutes, close your eyes and notice the manner in which what you are with in the Natural World now lives within the place of the heart. There may be light, or an image, or movement, most certainly strong feeling.

While present with that inner imagining of a specific aspect of the Natural World, have attention focused in the heart — and in an act of active-receptivity, allow the feeling within the heart to flow into the inner attentiveness. With a very, very gentle act of the will, increase the intensity of that heart-feeling flowing into the inner attentiveness, through rhythmically breathing this heart-feeling into the attentiveness. This heart-feeling is not an emotion; it is a strongly felt "urgency" of love within the heart, as if there is an unending force within the heart that is autonomous from you, though also the most intimate aspect of you. Attentiveness does not occur outside the heart either; it is not as if the forces of attention are looking on to what goes on within the heart. Heart-attentiveness seems to inhere within the heart, but can be felt as a force that, while in inner connection with the heart's imagining, can also affect it.

Notice what begins to occur. When the inner attentiveness is approached from love within the heart, and love approaches attentiveness, the inner presence, the felt image of what or who we're with, responds. Warmth can be felt within the heart, and the warmth increases, maybe even warming the body. This warmth permates and embraces the image being held within the heart. An attraction forms between the warmed image and the felt sense of light within the heart, and in that moment, we feel that the image-presence is also a world presence. Invisible, but palpably present. It is as if the released image now finds its relation with the wholeness of the world, and this occurrence is the world action of the heart.

Do this practice in some sort of rhythm — once a day at the same time, for example. Do it for a month, maybe two, until there comes a point when it seems to live within you, has become a part of your very being.

23. Cleaning the Memory Mirror of Sensing Earth

Sense-feeling of Earth-soul requires loosening the ways that immediate perceiving is always guided by what we already know. We know, for example, "what trees are." This knowing completely pervades our perceiving.

On a walk, find a place that attracts you. Walk rather aimlessly and without a goal in mind; you will notice some particular aspect of the world that the body feels in connection with — a stone, a plant, a flower, a tree, grass, a plant.

In that place, attend to all that you can notice — everything that you take in through sensory presence.

See-feel-heart-smell — notice colors, weight, alignment, movement, stillness, light — and try to take it in all at once, rather than piecemeal.

Notice both the exterior objects and what you are sensing, and any feelings you may experience, any images or fantasies, intuition, memories, whatever occurs.

Begin to inwardly slowly strip away, one at a time, the characteristics of what you sensed and felt — strip away the "what" of what you sensed. For example, if you felt the particularity of a certain tree, now strip away the tree as it exists within your experience; strip away the colors seen, the sounds heard, the movements seen and felt, the memories, the images, the fantasies, down to the felt presence of Earth — down to that ever-present "place" where you always are. Strip away everything you can possibly imagine that connects you with matter. Let all this collapse into nothing.

Stay as long as possible with the nothing. Feel the Silence.

Now, place attention within the heart and feel the Silence — allow all that was stripped away to now be heart-present within the Silence.

24. Bearing the Travails of Earth

Begin with inward presence with some devastating event — a large forest fire, a tsunami, oil spill, water contamination, poaching tigers or elephants . . . whatever first comes to you.

Be inwardly present with such a moment through inner images. Allow yourself to enter into the images . . . become the images, feel the grieving . . . it is yours and also it is Earth's. You can best feel such images from within heart-presence and the Silence, and at the same time, with attention placed in the region of the feet. You will feel currents emerging from the Earth, and shortly qualities of grieving will be felt. Then, allow the felt grief to be filled with a specific image of what Earth bears.

Allow the felt image, with the grieving, to come to the inner surface of the heart.

Notice that a stilling of the disturbing images occurs. Disturbance is not blocked out, denied, or removed. The stilling holds all of the qualities of the images, but now in the Stillness of the heart instead of the trembling of emotion. Stay within this stillness of images for a while.

Then, allow your attention to be with the stillness of the images, and with your attentiveness, the soft will of attentiveness, move the image-complex to the center of the heart. Feel the images right at the center of the heart. It takes little effort for this movement to take place. If you find that it takes effort, you are likely now, in attentiveness, within the images, but have distanced yourself from them and are as if "looking at them." Go back to the previous step, and proceed again.

At the center of the heart lies a quality of "golden light." It may not be actually "light," but it has the feeling quality of golden light — warm, soft, bright, filled with levity. Again, the devastating images are not erased. They are now bathed in the qualities of the center of the heart, and now, even within this "darkness," a creative force can be noticed. Stay here for a while.

Then, allow your attention to be at the back of the heart. The back of the heart feels like the opening to an unending vortex with the felt quality of the action of love. It is not sentimental or emotional love, but rather the force of love. Allow the images, with soft attentiveness, to move into the depth at the back of the heart. Stay there for a while.

Then, begin to allow the images to move, first, from the back of the heart. The images feel decidedly different. Filled with creative force. Then, allow the images to move into the golden light at the center of the heart. The images garner levity there, and are felt again as belonging here, with the Earth, whereas at the back of the heart, all goes into depth-force.

Then, allow the images to move to the surface of the heart. The devastation of the images has not gone away, it is still present — now you bear what is happening, but it does not feel that you are bearing the devastation alone. Sometimes when there is great ardor of heart with this practice, at this place of the inner surface of the heart, visions of your particular engagement with the healing of Earth appear and can be felt.

SOME READINGS

Henry Corbin
  Alone with the Alone
  Spiritual Body and Celestial Earth
  The Man of Light in Iranian Sufism
  Temple and Contemplation

Robert Sardello
  Silence: The Mystery of Wholeness
  Love and the Soul: Creating a Future for Earth

Peter Selg
  The Mystery of the Heart

Rudolf Steiner:
  Isis Mary Sophia: Her Mission and Ours
  Start Now! A Book of Soul and Spiritual Exercises
  The Book of Revelation: And the Work of the Priest
  Mystics of the Renaissance: And Their Relation to Modern Thought
  Youth and the Etheric Heart:
      Rudolf Steiner Speaks to the Younger Generation

Dennis Klocek

The Seer's Handbook: A Guide to Higher Perception

Seeking Spirit Vision: Essays on Developing Imagination

Marko Pogacnik

Gaia's Quantum Leap:

    A Guide to Living Through the Coming Earth Changes

Nature Spirits and Elemental Beings:

    Working with the Intelligence in Nature

Arthur Zajonc

Meditation as Contemplative Inquiry

Renée Coleman

Icons of a Dreaming Heart: The Art and Practice of Dream-Centered Living

James Finley

The Contemplative Heart

Cynthia Bourgeault

Centering Prayer and Inner Awakening

Richard Rohr

The Naked Now: Learning to See as the Mystics See

Paul Emberson
From Gondhishapur to Silicon Valley, Vol. II

R. J. Stewart
The Sphere of Art
The Sphere of Art II

Jacob Lorber
Earth and Moon

Satprem
The Mind of the Cells: Willed Mutation of Our Species

Bernadette Roberts
The Experience of No-Self: A Contemplative Journey

Christopher Vasey
Spiritual Mysteries of the Blood

Penney Peirce
Leap of Perception: The Transforming Power of Your Attention
Frequency: The Power of Personal Vibration

Pier Luigi Ighina
The Magnetic Atom

Robert Sardello is Co-Director, with Cheryl Sanders-Sardello, of the School of Spiritual Psychology.

www.heartfulsoul.com

Printed in Poland
by Amazon Fulfillment
Poland Sp. z o.o., Wrocław

32352188R00170